Contents

Grammar Focus

Use with student text page 12.

Use Present Continuous Tense Verbs

SUBJECT	*BE*	VERB + *–ING*
I	am	reading.
You	are	learning.
We	are	studying.
They	are	practicing.
Jim and Sue	are	writing.
He	is	eating.
She	is	sitting.
It	is	sleeping.
Jim	is	standing.

LANGUAGE NOTES:

1. If a verb is one syllable and ends in a vowel + one consonant (swim, sit), double the consonant and add *–ing* (swimming, sitting).
2. If a verb ends in a consonant + *e* (lose, live), drop the *-e* and add *–ing* (losing, living).
3. For most verbs that end in an *i* + *e* (die, lie), change the *i* + *e* to a *y* and add *–ing* (dying, lying).
4. Just add *–ing* to most other verbs (walking, helping)
5. To form the negative, put *not* after the verb *am / is / are:*
   Dan *is not* writing a composition.   I am *not* sleeping in class.

EXAMPLES	USE
Dan *is writing* a letter to his family now. It is *snowing* now.	To show that an action is in progress at this moment.
Dan and his brother *are gaining* weight. Dan *is writing* a term paper this semester.	To show a long-term action that is in progress but may not be happening at this exact moment.
He *is wearing* a sweater. He *is sitting* near the window.	To describe a state or condition using verbs such as *sit, stand, wear,* or *sleep.*

Grammar Practice A

VISIONS
Language ✦ Literature ✦ Content

THOMSON
HEINLE

Australia ✦ Canada ✦ Mexico ✦ Singapore ✦ United Kingdom ✦ United States

Visions A Grammar Practice

Publisher: *Phyllis Dobbins*

Director of Content Development: *Anita Raducanu*

Editorial Assistant: *Emily Dendinger*

Executive Marketing Manager: *James McDonough*

Director of Product Marketing: *Amy T. Mabley*

Production Editor: *Dawn Marie Elwell*

Senior Print Buyer: *Marcia Locke*

Development Editor: *Monica Glina*

Compositor: *ICC Macmillan Inc.*

Project Manager: *Parul Arya*

Cover Designer: *Lori Stuart*

Printer: *Thomson West*

Printed in the United States of America.
  2 3 4 5 6 7 8 9 10 – 10 09 08 07

For more information contact Thomson Heinle, 25 Thomson Place, Boston, Massachusetts 02210 USA,
or you can visit our Internet site at elt.thomson.com

ISBN-13: 978-1-4240-0571-0
ISBN-10: 1-4240-0571-X

Name _____ Date _____

EXERCISE 1 Write the *-ing* form of the verb.

Example: cook _cooking_

1. walk _walking_
2. talk _talking_
3. use _using_
4. exercise _exercising_
5. say _saying_
6. do _doing_

7. turn _turning_
8. set _setting_
9. happen _happening_
10. taste _tasting_
11. think _thinking_
12. run _running_

EXERCISE 2 Circle the correct present continuous verb in each sentence.

Example: She deciding / (is deciding) what to do.

1. The Jones family are worrying / is worrying about the rent.

2. He are drinking / is drinking hot chocolate.

3. You are reading / read your homework every night this week.

4. Jane is working / working all day.

5. We is having / are having a good time at our job.

6. Those people is waiting / are waiting for the bus.

7. The fish swimming / are swimming up the river.

8. The baseball player is laughing / be laughing at the other team.

9. I are doing / am doing my grammar exercises tonight.

10. It is rain / is raining right now.

11. Our baseball team is winning / are winning today.

12. The hot dog vendor is selling / selling many hot dogs with onions.

EXERCISE 3 Fill in the missing part of each sentence.

Example: He is eat _ing_ a sandwich.

They _are_ playing baseball.

1. I am think _ing_ of you.
2. My mother and father _are_ riding the train.
3. Karla _is_ wearing a new dress.
4. The students in my class are speak _ing_ English.
5. He is learn _ing_ Chinese.
6. My teacher _is_ writing on the board.
7. I _am_ taking notes.
8. The boats _are_ sailing on the water.
9. The sun _is_ shining down.
10. My brother is study _ing_ computer science.

EXERCISE 4 Write a sentence in the present continuous tense using the words given.

Example: the cat / sleep _The cat is sleeping._

1. my brother / cook / dinner _My brother is cooking dinner._
2. my sister / talk / on the telephone _My sister is talking on the phone._
3. my father / use / his computer _My father is using his computer._
4. my mother / exercise _My mother is exercising._
5. the dog / eat _The dog is eatting._
6. I / do / my homework _I'm doing my homework_
7. the earth / turn _The earth is turning_
8. the sun / set _The sun is setting._
9. plants / grow _the plants are growing._
10. I / think / about my friend _I'm thinking about my friend._

EXERCISE 5 Answer each question using the present continuous tense with true information about yourself.

Example: Who is helping you with your homework?

My friend Lee is helping me with my homework.

1. What are you doing now? _I am writting on the book_
2. What are you thinking about? _I'm thinking about my friends._

Name _____ Date _____

3. Where are you sitting? _I'm sitting on the front._
4. What are you writing with? _I'm writing with my pencil._
5. Is anyone sitting near you? _Someone is sitting near me._
6. Who is teaching you English (this semester)? _I don't know._
7. What other classes are you taking? _I'm taking sport class._
8. What are you wearing? _I'm wearing my shirts._
9. Are you sleeping? _No, I'm not sleeping_
10. Are you eating? _No, I'm not eating._

EXERCISE 6 Fill in the missing part of each sentence.

Example: You ___are___ eating dinner.

1. Carol is do _ing_ the dishes.
2. The brothers are play _ing_ basketball.
3. The kids _are_ watch _ing_ cartoons.
4. It is snow _ing_ right now.
5. My mom is wash _ing_ the dog.

6. You _are_ read _ing_ that book for English class.
7. I _'m_ rent _ing_ this video.
8. He _is_ go _ing_ to school.
9. She _is_ still sleep _ing_.
10. You _are_ wear _ing_ green socks.

EXERCISE 7 Rewrite each sentence in the negative form.

Example: The girl is jogging.
The girl is not jogging.

1. The professor is writing. _____
2. He is leaving. _____
3. The leaves are turning brown. _____
4. Jorge is studying English. _____
5. The audience is applauding. _____
6. The fans are cheering. _____
7. The flowers are blooming. _____
8. The stores are opening early. _____
9. The sun is shining. _____
10. People are celebrating! _____

Grammar Focus

Use with student text page 24.

Identify Subjects and Verbs in Sentences

EXAMPLE	EXPLANATION
S V Bob likes Mary. S V We like movies.	The subject (S) comes before the verb (V).
S V S V Bob likes Mary because she helps him.	There can be more than one subject (S) in a sentence.
S V S V I like movies because they entertain me.	There can be more than one verb (V) in a sentence.

LANGUAGE NOTES:

1. The subject of a sentence is the word or phrase that performs the action.
2. The verb is the action the subject performs.
3. There can be more than one subject or verb in a sentence.

    S   S V
    Dogs and cats are favorite pets.

    S   V   V
    She walks and jogs for exercise.

EXERCISE 1   Write *S* or *V* over the subject and verb in each sentence.

         S   V
Example: She smells the roses.

  S V
1. I eat bananas.

   S   V
2. Michael knows Dorothy.

 S V   S
3. He is a doctor.

    S   V
4. They have money.

       S   V
5. She makes hats.

      S   S   V
6. Maggie and Tim grow vegetables.

  S V
7. It is a fluffy cloud.

    S   V
8. We love English.

EXERCISE 2 Fill in the blank with a subject to complete each sentence.

good

Example: *Chen* wears nice clothes.

1. _Ms. Wall_ speaks English well.
2. _David_ has a car.
3. _Ryan_ likes classical music.
4. _He_ reads many books.
5. _She_ is never late to class.

6. _She_ takes good notes.
7. _Benny_ has a job.
8. _He_ helps me study.
9. _She_ has a nice smile.
10. _She_ does homework.

EXERCISE 3 Circle the subject and underline the verb in each sentence.

Example: (I) always <u>pay</u> cash at the supermarket.

1. (Dexter's Books) <u>sells</u> maps.

2. (My aunt) rarely <u>stays</u> in a hotel.

3. Where do (you) usually <u>go</u> shopping?

4. (Her hair) <u>is</u> brown.

5. (My mother) <u>calls</u> me every Sunday.

6. In Japan, (people) <u>keep money</u> at the post office.

7. Does the (Ramirez family) <u>live</u> in Buenos Aires?

8. (My brother) <u>is</u> in second grade.

EXERCISE 4 Write *S* or *V* over the subjects and verbs in this paragraph.

Example: The fog covers the city.

Weather affects everyone. Some people love bad weather, and some people hate bad weather. In the city, businessmen and businesswomen use umbrellas in the rain. The umbrellas keep them from getting wet. In the city, people dislike the rain. People on vacation don't like rain. Rain keeps people inside. People play sports outside on vacation, and rain stops outdoor baseball games and basketball games.

EXERCISE 5 Write *S* or *V* over the subject and verb in each sentence.

               S   V

Example: The bird sings a song.

          S   V

1. The family makes dinner in the kitchen.

        S   V

2. My brother takes a shower in the small bathroom.

        S   V

3. The house has five bedrooms.

       S   V

4. The white car is in the green garage.

       S   V

5. The mover put the coffee table in the hall.

       S   V

6. The brothers need to buy furniture for the house.

    S   S   V

7. John and Jane want to rent a new house, but it is very expensive.

       S V V

8. The cat is under the sofa in the living room.

EXERCISE 6 Circle the subjects and underline the verbs in these sentences.

Example: My (aunt and uncle) live and work in a retirement community.

1. My (uncle) works for a (company) that builds (condominiums).

2. (My aunt) decorates and sells the condominiums.

3. My (aunt and uncle) also participate in the (clubhouse) activities.

4. (They) interview and schedule entertainment for the community residents.

5. The (community residents) enjoy the fine musicians that my (aunt and uncle) hire.

EXERCISE 7 Write *S* or *V* over the subject and verb in each sentence.

              S   V
Example: People collect many different things.

1. Andrew owns a wonderful collection of stamps.

2. Gianna and Kurt buy and sell rare CDs.

3. Andrew researches and purchases three new stamps a month.

4. Gianna and Kurt visit specialty music stores.

5. Gianna and Kurt trade a CD for a limited-edition stamp.

6. They wrap and deliver the limited-edition stamp to Andrew.

7. Andrew thanks and hugs his friends, Gianna and Kurt, for his present.

EXERCISE 8 Circle the subjects and underline the verbs in this paragraph.

(Example) Bruce and his sister, Lisa, have a passion for shopping. Every weekend, they buy the newspaper. They sort and read the ads to see which stores have the best sales. Clothes, shoes, electronic items, and specialty foods interest them the most. They compare and record the prices of these items.

    Sometimes, Bruce and Lisa call and invite their friends, David and Shanti, to go shopping with them. David and Shanti love shopping, too. They don't research the price of an item, though. Instead, they use a different method. They read and analyze information that tells them about the quality of the item. Many times, Bruce and Lisa find a product for a good price, and David and Shanti find the same product based on its quality!

Name _____ Date _____

Grammar Focus

Use with student text page 40.

Use Subject Pronouns

NOUN	SUBJECT PRONOUN	COMPLEMENT
I	**I**	am happy.
the man	**He**	is married.
my mother	**She**	has curly hair.
the map	**It**	is new.
the dog	**It**	is friendly.
my friend and I	**We**	speak Spanish.
you	**You** (singular)	are a good friend.
	You (plural)	are good friends.
the students	**They**	are new students.
the shoes	**They**	are brown.

- **I, he, she, it, we, you,** and **they** are subject pronouns. They replace nouns.
- **You** is both singular and plural.
- **It** is used for singular nouns (animals and things).
- **They** is used for plural nouns (people, animals, and things).

EXERCISE 1 Roberto is talking about his English class. Write a pronoun in each blank.

Example: Hi, my name is <u>Roberto</u>. _____*I*_____ am very happy in my new class.

1. The <u>teacher</u> is Mrs. Edwards. ____She____ is very kind.
2. <u>My classmates and I</u> work hard. ____They____ are good students.
3. <u>Rieko and Tatsuya</u> are from Japan. ____They____ are nice.
4. <u>Felipe</u> is a young man. ____He____ is not married.
5. I like <u>the books</u> in my class. ____They____ are very interesting.
6. The teacher gives us <u>homework</u>. ____It____ is difficult.
7. <u>Duong and Nam</u> are my classmates. ____They____ are from Vietnam.
8. <u>Nam</u> is a nice boy. ____He____ has a sister.

EXERCISE 2 Fill in each blank with the correct pronoun.

Example: Daniel and Yoshio are students. _____ *They* _____ are students.

1. The pencil is lost. _____ It _____ is lost.
2. Julie is a doctor. _____ She _____ is a doctor.
3. The mother is asleep. _____ She _____ is asleep.
4. The father is in his room. _____ He _____ is in his room.
5. My brother and I like sports. _____ We _____ like sports.
6. My cousins are in Mexico. _____ They _____ are in Mexico.
7. Amy is my favorite singer. _____ She _____ is my favorite singer.
8. Joshua is a hard worker. _____ He _____ is a hard worker.
9. Karen and Lisa are my best friends. _____ They _____ are my best friends.
10. Tom and Paul aren't friends. _____ They _____ aren't friends.
11. Donald is my teacher. _____ he _____ is my teacher.
12. Bombay is in India. _____ It _____ is in India.
13. Carrots and potatoes are vegetables. _____ They _____ are vegetables.
14. You and I are so happy together. _____ We _____ are so happy together.
15. Maria is a dancer. _____ She _____ is a dancer.
16. Your English is very good. _____ it _____ is very good.
17. I am tired. _____ I _____ am tired.
18. Tim and Allen are brothers. _____ They _____ are brothers.
19. My uncle is on vacation in Hawaii. _____ He _____ is on vacation in Hawaii.
20. The cat and the dog are good friends. _____ They _____ are good friends.
21. My mother is a teacher. _____ She _____ is a teacher.
22. You and I are from the same school. _____ We _____ are from the same school.
23. English is a difficult language. _____ It _____ is a difficult language.
24. France and Italy are countries. _____ They _____ are countries.
25. Rome is a city. _____ It _____ is a city.

EXERCISE 3 Complete each sentence. Use a pronoun.

Example: Amal is a student. _____*He*_____ is from Egypt.

1. Elsa is a student. _____She_____ is from Russia.
2. Amal and I are students. _____we_____ are in the same class.
3. Mr. Jackson is a teacher. _____He_____ is from Florida.
4. Mrs. Samuel and Mr. Jackson are from Florida. _____They_____ are teachers.

EXERCISE 4 Circle the correct answer in each sentence.

Example: He /(We) are good friends.

1. (It)/ She is cold and rainy today.
2. They /(I) am in the house right now.
3. (They)/ He are at home with me.
4. We /(It) is time for dinner.
5. (It)/ She is a city in Europe.
6. It /(We) are on vacation.
7. (It)/ You is really interesting.
8. We /(They) are big countries.
9. You /(He) is my best friend.
10. (They)/ It are my favorite colors.

11. They /(It) is delicious.
12. He /(They) are in the same class.
13. (I)/ You am a student.
14. He /(It) is about 4:00 A.M.
15. (We)/ He are cousins.
16. (She)/ You is a doctor.
17. We /(They) are difficult languages.
18. (It)/ He is a big city.
19. You /(He) are at school.
20. They /(She) is interesting.

EXERCISE 5 Substitute each subject pronoun with nouns.

Example: We are on a trip to New York City.

My friends and I are on a trip to New York City.

1. They live in Australia.

Mark and Jon live in Australia.

2. He is a teacher.

   Mr. Summit is a teacher.

3. She is from Argentina.

   ____Maria____ is from Argentina.

4. It is a small school.

   ___elementary___ is a small school.

5. It is far away.

   ___New york___ is far away.

6. He works at home.

   ____Mike____ works at home.

7. She looks 25 years old.

   ___Ashley___ looks 25 years old.

8. We came from China.

   My friend and I came from China.

EXERCISE 6 Substitute a pronoun for each underlined noun. Write the pronoun on the line.

Example: Barry asked if Ken had eaten lunch yet. _He_

1. Tammy said that she didn't think so. _She_
2. Barry and Tammy decided that they should all eat together. _They_
3. Barry called Ken. _He_
4. "Would you like to have lunch with Tammy and me?" _Us_
5. "Well, lunch is an important meal." Ken thought to himself. _it_
6. Ken exclaimed, "I thought you'd never ask!" _He_
7. Barry, Tammy, and Ken met at their favorite spot for lunch. _They_
8. "I'm glad we could all have lunch together," Tammy said. _She_

Grammar Focus

Use with student text page 52.

Use the Verb *To Be* with Complements

	FORM OF *BE*	COMPLEMENT	EXPLANATION
I	am	a doctor.	A complement can be a noun.
You	are	a winner.	
Boston	is	a city.	A noun is a person, place, thing, or idea.
The stove	is	hot.	An adjective is a word that describes a noun or pronoun.
She	is	intelligent.	
We	are	excited.	
The flowers	are	beautiful.	A complement can be an adjective.

LANGUAGE NOTES:

1. A complement describes or renames the subject of a sentence.
2. A complement can be a noun or an adjective.
3. A complement can follow a form of the verb *to be*. These forms include *am, is,* and *are.*

EXERCISE 1 Underline the form of *to be* in each sentence below.

Example: He <u>is</u> a painter.

1. I <u>am</u> a student.
2. I <u>am</u> 15 years old.
3. My father <u>is</u> a businessman.
4. He <u>is</u> always busy.
5. My mother <u>is</u> a teacher.
6. She <u>is</u> intelligent.
7. New York <u>is</u> exciting.
8. It <u>is</u> cold in the winter.
9. What time <u>is</u> it? It <u>is</u> 5:15.
10. We <u>are</u> in Mexico.
11. You <u>are</u> my friend.
12. You <u>are</u> tall.
13. Dogs <u>are</u> animals.
14. Italy and Spain <u>are</u> countries.
15. My sister <u>is</u> a doctor.
16. They <u>are</u> children.
17. Dogs and cats <u>are</u> good pets.
18. She <u>is</u> funny.
19. My mother <u>is</u> beautiful.
20. He <u>is</u> my best friend.
21. They <u>are</u> classmates.
22. My brother <u>is</u> a lawyer.

Name _____ Date _____

EXERCISE 2 Write *V* (for verb) or *C* (for complement) over the form of *to be* and the complement in each sentence.

   V   C
Example: China is in Asia.

1. You are happy.

2. I am friendly.

3. January and February are cold.

4. It is hot today.

5. It is 4:45 P.M.

6. He is 16 years old.

7. A fly is an insect.

8. She is pretty.

9. Dr. Jones is a dentist.

10. You are 14 years old.

11. It is lunchtime.

12. Brazil is a beautiful country.

13. They are very sad.

14. I am a driving teacher.

EXERCISE 3 Circle the form of *to be* and underline the complement in each sentence below.

Example: Eva (is) Polish.

1. Duong is bored.

2. Eva is short.

3. My eyes are green.

4. My hair is straight.

5. You are early.

6. We are sisters.

7. I am at work.

8. They are Cuban.

EXERCISE 4 Write *V* or *C* over the form of *to be* and the complement in each sentence.

                  V   C

Example: She is not lonely.

1. We are not married.

2. I am not tall.

3. You are not students.

4. They are not Silvia's parents.

5. It is not Carla's computer.

6. We are not single.

7. He is not bald.

8. You are not late.

EXERCISE 5 Write 10 sentences in which the complement is a noun.

Example: *Donna is a nurse.*

1. Raymond doesn't like eggs.

2. John has enormous strength.

3. Tom is a general.

4. Ivan play computer games everyday

5. Most people have a garden in their backyard

6. _____

7. _____

8. _____

9. _____

10. _____

VISIONS A Grammar Practice • Copyright © Thomson Heinle

Name _____ Date _____

Write 8 sentences in which the complement is an adjective.

Example: *The news is exciting.*

1. This school is so great.
2. The home work was difficult.
3. The people are different.
4. He is ridiculous.
5. The melted bubble gum was jammy.
6. _____
7. _____
8. _____

EXERCISE 6 Look at the sentences you wrote for Exercise 5. Write *V* or *C* over the form of *to be* and the complement in each one of your sentences.

        V   C

Example: Donna is a nurse.

EXERCISE 7 Write each complement on the blank line.

Example: Hobbies are fun. _____fun_____

1. Gardening is a popular hobby. ___hobby___
2. For many, it is relaxing. ___relaxing___
3. People who garden are patient. ___patient___
4. They are excited when spring comes. ___comes___
5. Spring is a perfect time to plant new flowers. ___flower___
6. Flowers are a colorful addition to a garden. ___garden___
7. Shrubs are also a popular choice. ___choice___
8. Trees are perfect for shade. ___shade___
9. Weeds are a nuisance. ___nuisance___
10. Gardening isn't boring! ___boring___

Grammar Focus

Use with student text page 66.

Recognize Possessive Nouns

NOUN	ENDING	EXAMPLE
Singular noun: father mother	Add apostrophe + *s*.	I use my **father's** last name. I don't use my **mother's** last name.
Plural noun ending in *s:* parents boys	Add apostrophe only.	My **parents'** names are Ethel and Herman. Ted and Mike are **boys'** names.
Irregular plural noun: children women	Add apostrophe + *s*.	What are your **children's** names? Marilyn and Sandra are **women's** names.
Names that end in *s:* Mr. Harris Charles	Add apostrophe + *s*.	Do you know **Mr. Harris's** wife? Do you know **Charles's** wife?

LANGUAGE NOTES:
1. Use the possessive form for people and other living things.
2. For inanimate objects, we usually use the form *the* _____ *of* _____.
   Washington College is the name of my school.

EXERCISE 1 Fill in each blank with the correct possessive form.

Example: My mom *'s* _____ cooking is even better than my grandma *'s* _____ cooking.

1. Stop! That is James _____ toothbrush.
2. Can you get me Ms. Reese _____ e-mail address?
3. Football players _____ uniforms are very hard to clean.
4. Your school _____ new Web site is really well designed.
5. Other schools _____ Web sites aren't nearly so attractive.
6. You'll find the dresses you want in the girls _____ department.
7. You should go to the children _____ shoe department.
8. Women _____ clothing is on the fourth floor.
9. Go to the third floor for men _____ clothing.
10. Children! Do not pull the cat _____ tail!

11. She is wearing her grandmother _____ diamond bracelet.

12. Everyone wants to go to John _____ party Saturday night.

13. Quick, hide the cake! I hear Daddy _____ footsteps!

14. Let me take a look at my brother _____ schedule.

15. Wait a minute. This is not Dr. Williams _____ signature.

16. Our English class is reading my favorite author _____ latest book.

17. Show us that picture of your family _____ new house.

18. The hurricane washed away many families _____ houses.

19. I cannot read my teacher _____ handwriting.

20. What are the political parties _____ views?

EXERCISE 2 Some of the following sentences can show possession with apostrophes (*'s* or *'*). Rewrite these sentences. Write "no change" for the others.

Example: The hat of my father is new. *My father's hat is new.* _____

The color of the house is white. *no change* _____

1. I always eat the dinners of my mother. _____

2. The name of this book is *Visions Grammar Practice*. _____

3. The name of my cat is Nemo. _____

4. What are the names of your best friends? _____

5. Who is the brother of Phyllis? _____

6. The roof of the house is white. _____

7. I like to go to the house of my friend. _____

8. New Language Center is the name of my school. _____

9. The toy of the baby is on the floor. _____

10. Where is the food of the children? _____

11. Red and blue are the favorite colors of my brother. _____

12. The color of the car is green. _____

13. This is the pen of my teacher. _____

14. The job of the doctor is to help sick people. _____

15. Do you live in the house of your parents? _____

16. The subject of this class is English. _____

17. The name of the mother of my best friend is Mabel. _____

18. The glass of the window is clear. _____

EXERCISE 3 Use the words to write a sentence that contains a possessive form. (The words are not always in the correct order.)

Example: the table / the leg / is broken

The leg of the table is broken. _____

1. where is / wallet / Papa

    _____

2. he is wearing / shirt / Dan

    _____

3. someone tore / cover / the book

    _____

4. the chair / the arm / is broken

    _____

EXERCISE 4 Write 10 sentences using words from the box below. Use the possessive form of the noun when possible. You can use other words, too.

my mother	car
my father	pen
my best friend	book
my sister/brother	clothes
my teacher	favorite color
my hometown	shoes
Andre	pet
Lee	name
Carlos	job
Jenna	game

Example: *My mother's favorite color is yellow.* _____

1. _____
2. _____
3. _____
4. _____
5. _____
6. _____
7. _____
8. _____
9. _____
10. _____

EXERCISE 5 Write the correct possessive form of each phrase.

Example: a dogs collar   _a dog's collar_

1. dogs (plural) collars   _____
2. schools (plural) reputations   _____
3. a kids bicycle   _____
4. kids (plural) bicycles   _____
5. a canvas texture   _____
6. a stores circulars   _____
7. stores (plural) circulars   _____
8. Mrs. Regis Dalmatian   _____
9. a students grades   _____
10. students (plural) grades   _____

EXERCISE 6 Write the correct possessive form of each word in parentheses.

Example: (Sonia) _Sonia's_ friend, Ross, is leaving for college.

1. (Ross) college is two hours from home.   _____
2. Ross drove his (parents) car to college.   _____
3. The (cars) gas tank needed to be filled.   _____
4. (His) (roommates) family helped with his luggage.   _____
5. Ross is taking Professor (Cross) class.   _____
6. His (professors) Web sites listed the required books for all of his classes.   _____
7. The (bookstores) hours are 9 to 5.   _____
8. His purchase almost exceeded his credit (cards) limit.   _____
9. He checked the dining (halls) menu.   _____
10. When he returned from dinner, his two new (neighbors) music was loud.   _____
11. His parents visited him during (parents) weekend.   _____
12. His (roommates) printer prints in color.   _____
13. His (sisters) letter arrived two days after classes started.   _____
14. The (letters) message was universal. All families are proud of their (childrens) achievements.   _____

Grammar Focus

Use with student text page 90.

Identify the Simple Present Tense

SUBJECT	BASE FORM	COMPLEMENT	SUBJECT	−S FORM	COMPLEMENT
I	need		He	needs	
You	need		She	needs	
We	need	water.	It	needs	water.
They	do not need		A plant	does not need	
Trees	don't need		A person	doesn't need	

EXAMPLE	USE
Cats **like** milk.	with general truths
Japanese people **bow** when they meet.	with customs
We **take** a vacation every summer.	to show regular or repeated actions or habits
He **comes** from Iraq.	to show places of origin

LANGUAGE NOTES:
1. Three verbs have an irregular –s form: *have / has, go / goes,* and *do / does.*
2. To form the negative, use *do* or *does* + *not* and the base form of the verb.

EXERCISE 1 Write the correct verb in each of the sentences below.

Example: George and Mary (need / needs) _____*need*_____ a new house.

1. Carlos (like / likes) _____ ice cream.
2. Tomoko (want / wants) _____ a new bicycle.
3. Many people (think / thinks) _____ it's good.
4. I (hate / hates) _____ parties.
5. They (go / goes) _____ to school on Saturdays.
6. Julia (come / comes) _____ from England.
7. Birds (fly / flies) _____ in the sky.
8. New York (have / has) _____ many tall buildings.
9. He (write / writes) _____ novels.
10. My family (watch / watches) _____ a lot of TV.

EXERCISE 2   Choose the correct form of the present tense. Fill in the correct bubble.

			A	B
Example: The car _____ a radio.	A. have	B. has	○	●
1. We _____ English in the evening.	A. practice	B. practices	○	○
2. The children _____ TV.	A. watch	B. watches	○	○
3. Tatsuya _____ Japanese.	A. speak	B. speaks	○	○
4. Silvia _____ to work at 8:00.	A. go	B. goes	○	○
5. My sisters _____ in Boston.	A. live	B. lives	○	○
6. The cat _____ TV.	A. like	B. likes	○	○
7. You _____ homework in the morning.	A. do	B. does	○	○
8. I _____ books.	A. like	B. likes	○	○

EXERCISE 3   Write the correct form of the verb. Then, finish each sentence with your own ideas.

Example: He (like) *likes our English class.* _____

1. I (live) _____
2. My family (live) _____
3. I (study) _____
4. My school (have) _____
5. My teacher (speak) _____
6. The students in my class (do) _____
7. Our classroom (have) _____
8. I (read) _____
9. My friend (read) _____
10. I (like) _____
11. My friend (want) _____
12. My family (go) _____

EXERCISE 4   Fill in each blank with the negative form of the underlined verb.

Example: My cousin Danielle <u>lives</u> in London.

        She _____ *doesn't live* _____ in San Francisco.

1. My cousin Danielle <u>comes</u> from England. She _____ from the United States.
2. She <u>lives</u> alone in London. She _____ with her parents.

3. Her parents <u>live</u> in Hastings. They _____ in London.

4. She <u>works</u> in London. She _____ in New York.

5. She <u>has</u> a lot of work. She _____ much free time.

6. Danielle <u>likes</u> classical music. She _____ popular music as much.

7. On weekends, Danielle <u>goes</u> to concerts. She _____ to discos.

8. Danielle <u>works</u> as a teacher. She _____ as a secretary.

9. She <u>eats</u> a lot of vegetables. She _____ meat.

10. She <u>wears</u> colorful clothes. She _____ black clothes.

EXERCISE 5 Change each sentence to the negative form.

Example: Minh speaks English in class.   *Minh doesn't speak English in class.*

1. Leo does homework every night.   _____

2. Minh and Leo listen to the teacher.   _____

3. Minh checks her work.   _____

4. Leo likes his classmates.   _____

5. Minh participates in class.   _____

6. Minh and Leo study at home.   _____

7. I practice English on the weekend.   _____

8. Minh and Leo watch TV in English.   _____

9. You talk to Leo.   _____

10. Leo answers questions.   _____

EXERCISE 6 Change each sentence to the negative form.

Example: I bite my fingernails. *I don't bite my fingernails.*

1. Marilyn comes from New Zealand. _____

2. Japan has many temples. _____

3. He eats his bread with butter. _____

4. French people go on vacation in August. _____

5. Noodles come from China. _____

6. Food costs money. _____

7. I go to the movies on weekends. _____

8. They play tennis together. _____

9. My teacher speaks English. _____

10. I come from Peru. _____

EXERCISE 7 Write affirmative or negative true statements about yourself.

Example: (speak French) *I don't speak French.* _____

1. (like sports) _____
2. (have a dog) _____
3. (eat breakfast every day) _____
4. (have a bicycle) _____
5. (like hot weather) _____
6. (speak Russian) _____
7. (have a job) _____
8. (go to discos) _____
9. (draw pictures) _____
10. (watch TV every night) _____
11. (stay up until midnight) _____
12. (call my family every week) _____

EXERCISE 8 Circle the verb in each sentence. Then rewrite each sentence in the negative form.

Example: Joseph (has) a notebook. *Joseph does not have a notebook.* _____

1. My mother reads the newspaper every day.

   _____

2. We study English grammar.

   _____

3. The teacher gives us homework.

   _____

4. The school has classrooms.

   _____

5. You drink water at break time.

   _____

6. The man speaks English at his job.

   _____

Grammar Focus

Use with student text page 104.

Identify and Punctuate Questions

YES / NO QUESTIONS	Wh- QUESTIONS	
Am I happy?	**Who** is from Japan?	**Who** are your brothers?
Are you married?	**What** is your name?	**What** are their names?
Is he tall?	**When** is your English class?	**When** am I busy?
Is she from Haiti?	**Why** is Gilberto always busy?	**Why** are we nervous?
Is it sunny today?	**Where** is my sister?	**Where** are you from?
Are we friends?	**How** is the weather today?	**How** are you today?
Are they in class?		
Do you need help?		
Do they speak French?		

LANGUAGE NOTES:

1. All questions end in a question mark.
2. A *wh-* word + *is* can form a contraction: *who's, what's, when's, why's, where's* and *how's.*
   Where's your homework?
   How's the weather?
   When's he getting here?
3. The verb *be* agrees with the subject of the sentence.
   What *is* your *name*?
   Where *are* your *books*?

| **EXERCISE 1** | Fill in each blank with the correct question word. |

Example: _What_____ is your name? My name is Lee.

1. _____ is Seoul? It's in Korea.
2. _____ is your birthday? It's in January.
3. _____ is your favorite singer? My favorite singer is Madonna.
4. _____ is a horse? A horse is an animal.
5. _____ are you late? I'm late because I missed the train.
6. _____ are your shoes? They are outside.
7. _____ is your sister? She's fine, thanks.
8. _____ is your homework? It's in my bag.

Name _____ Date _____

EXERCISE 2 All of these are questions. Put the words in the correct order. End each question with a question mark (?).

Example: Australians / English / speak / do _Do Australians speak English?_

1. Russia / a big country / is _____
2. Mexicans / Spanish / speak / do _____
3. do / know / you / college math _____
4. the Earth / very large / is _____
5. your friends / does / visit / she _____

EXERCISE 3 Use the words to ask a *yes / no* question. End each question with a question mark.

Example: Kenji / from Japan _Is Kenji from Japan?_

1. Anya and Ivan / from Russia _____
2. you / from Korea _____
3. I / late for class _____
4. Marie / from Haiti _____
5. we / busy today _____
6. Gilberto and Mario / tall _____
7. Mario / from Mexico _____
8. Kenji / at school _____

EXERCISE 4 Read each answer (A) below. Then, complete the question (Q) with the correct *wh-* question word + a form of *be*.

Example: **Q:** _Where is_ _____ Kenji from? **A:** Kenji is from Japan.

1. **Q:** _____ his sister's name? **A:** His sister's name is Miyuki.
2. **Q:** _____ his brothers' names? **A:** His brothers' names are Genki and Akira.
3. **Q:** _____ Kenji's parents? **A:** Kenji's parents are Ayumi and Takuya.
4. **Q:** _____ his grandparents? **A:** His grandparents are in Japan.
5. **Q:** _____ Kenji in English class? **A:** Kenji is in English class on Tuesday.
6. **Q:** _____ Kenji's English class? **A:** Kenji's English class is in the high school.
7. **Q:** _____ Kenji's teacher? **A:** Kenji's teacher is Mr. Brown.
8. **Q:** _____ Kenji today? **A:** Kenji is happy.
9. **Q:** _____ Kenji happy? **A:** Because he is going to the beach.
10. **Q:** _____ the weather today? **A:** It is sunny and warm.

EXERCISE 5 Read each statement. Then write a *yes / no* question about the words in parentheses ( ). Write or finish the short answer.

Example: China is a big country.

(England) *Is England a big country?* _____

Answer: *No, it isn't.* _____

1. Indonesia is a warm country.

(Iceland) _____

Answer: *No,* _____

2. French people eat a lot of cheese.

(Japanese people) _____

Answer: *No,* _____

3. Trains in Tokyo run on time.

(trains in your city) _____

Answer: *Yes,* _____

4. Mexican food is spicy.

(Korean food) _____

Answer: *Yes,* _____

5. Brazilians speak Portuguese.

(Argentineans) _____

Answer: *No,* _____

6. Soccer is popular in Japan.

(baseball) _____

Answer: *Yes,* _____

7. You study grammar.

(history) _____

Answer: *Yes,* _____

Name _____ Date _____

EXERCISE 6 Turn each statement into a question using a *wh-* question word.

Example: _What is a rose?_____ A rose is a flower.

1. _____ Red is a color.
2. _____ My birthday is in February.
3. _____ Life in New York is exciting.
4. _____ Vietnam is in Asia.
5. _____ He's from Turkey.
6. _____ My teacher is Ms. Sands.
7. _____ It's cold today.
8. _____ She's smart because she studies hard.
9. _____ I'm fine, thanks.
10. _____ My pens are on my desk.
11. _____ My name is Maria.
12. _____ His birthday is on July 3.

EXERCISE 7 Unscramble the words below to form questions.

Example: you / do / in the morning / what / eat
_What do you eat in the morning?_____

1. does / when / letters / write / he

   _____

2. she / does / go / after school / where

   _____

3. do / when / English / practice / you

   _____

4. how often / your friends / e-mail / you / do

   _____

5. is / who / film actor / your favorite

   _____

6. want / you / to leave / do / when

   _____

Grammar Focus

Use with student text page 116.

Identify Object Pronouns

SUBJECT	OBJECT PRONOUN	EXAMPLE SUBJECT	VERB	OBJECT PRONOUN
I	me	You	love	me.
you	you	I	love	you.
he	him	She	loves	him.
she	her	He	loves	her.
it	it	We	love	it.
we	us	They	love	us.
they	them	We	love	them.

LANGUAGE NOTES:

1. Use an object pronoun to substitute for an object noun:
   I love my mother. I visit *her* once a week.
2. Use *them* for plural people and things:
   I have two brothers. You know *them*.
3. An object pronoun can follow a preposition:
   My sister has a son. She always talks about *him*.

EXERCISE 1 Fill in each blank with the object pronoun of the underlined word or words.

Example: I eat ice cream. I eat *it* _____.

1. I see stars at night. I see _____ at night.

2. You help your brother. You help _____.

3. He cleans the garage. He cleans _____.

4. We like chicken very much. We like _____ very much.

5. They need a two-bedroom apartment. They need _____.

6. I open boxes at work. I open _____ at work.

7. She writes a composition. She writes _____.

8. It hits the car suddenly. It hits _____ suddenly.

9. The trees drop their leaves in fall. The trees drop _____ in fall.

10. He loves his mom very much. He loves _____ very much.

11. My mother often calls you. My mother often calls _____.

12. Every year he promises Julia and me. Every year he promises _____.

EXERCISE 2 Substitute a pronoun for the underlined words. Write each pronoun on the line.

Example: Amelia visits <u>new places</u> often.   *them*

1. Amelia loves <u>exotic places</u>.   _____

2. She spent <u>her last vacation</u> on a tropical island.   _____

3. She plans <u>her trips</u> thoroughly.   _____

4. First, she considers <u>possible destinations</u>.   _____

5. After considering <u>her options</u>, she chooses one.   _____

6. She informs <u>Mark</u>, her travel agent.   _____

7. Mark gives <u>Amelia</u> information about the destination.   _____

8. Amelia uses <u>the information</u> to make vacation plans.   _____

9. Amelia tells <u>Mark</u> about her final decision.   _____

10. Mark arranges <u>the flight and hotel</u> for Amelia.   _____

11. Amelia uses <u>the Internet</u> to research things to do on her vacation. _____

12. She buys <u>travel books</u>.   _____

13. The information and photographs in the books excite <u>Amelia</u>. _____

14. She always takes <u>pictures</u>.   _____

15. She shares <u>her pictures</u> with Mark.   _____

16. She usually brings <u>Mark</u> a souvenir, too.   _____

17. As soon as she returns home, she happily anticipates <u>another new and exotic place</u>. _____

18. She is already marking <u>pages</u> in the travel magazine for her next trip. _____

19. She calls <u>Mark</u> to discuss yet another trip.   _____

EXERCISE 3 Circle each object. Then substitute the object with a object pronoun.

Example: Davis planned (a party) for his birthday.   *it*

1. He invited his friends to the party.   _____

2. He mailed the invitations from the post office.   _____

3. Davis made a reservation at his favorite restaurant. _____

4. Gary bought a book and a CD for Davis. _____

5. Gary called Kayla about the cake. _____

6. Kayla ordered a cake for the party. _____

7. The restaurant billed Gary and Kayla for the cake. _____

8. Sidney wrapped Gary's present in blue wrapping paper. _____

9. Davis thanked Gary, Kayla, Andrew, and Sidney for coming to the party. _____

10. Gary, Kayla, Andrew, and Sidney congratulated Davis on his milestone. _____

11. After the party, Andrew and Sidney drove Kayla to her house. _____

12. Davis enjoyed his time with his friends. _____

EXERCISE 4   Underline each object and replace it with an object pronoun.

Example: Mrs. Engle gave her students a homework assignment.   _____*them*_____

1. Jonah reviewed the questions for the assignment. _____

2. He checked his practice schedule. _____

3. The schedule puzzled Jonah. _____

4. Practice usually includes the members of his team. _____

5. This week's schedule excluded his team. _____

6. Jonah likes basketball. _____

7. Jonah respects Mrs. Engle. _____

8. Jonah also takes Mrs. Engle's class seriously. _____

9. He asked his teammates, Harry and Blake, for some advice. _____

10. Harry and Blake advised Jonah to ask the coach. _____

11. After class, the boys found Coach Evans. _____

12. Coach Evans told Jonah, Harry, and Blake that they were not scheduled for practice that afternoon. _____

13. Coach Evans encouraged Jonah, Harry, and Blake to do their homework. _____

14. They completed the questions on the worksheets. _____

15. They each submitted an assignment. _____

16. Their work impressed Mrs. Engle. _____

17. Mrs. Engle commended Jonah, Harry, and Blake for work well done. _____

EXERCISE 5 Fill in each blank with the object pronoun of the underlined word or words.

Example: I understand you, and you understand *me* _____.

1. <u>Romeo</u> loves Juliet, and she loves _____, too.

2. <u>I</u> take care of my parents, and my parents take care of _____.

3. Her name is <u>Elizabeth</u>, but we call _____ Beth.

4. I like <u>sushi</u>. Do you like _____ too?

5. I speak <u>English</u> in class, but I don't speak _____ at home.

6. John walks toward <u>George</u> and looks at _____.

7. These are our <u>photo albums</u>. Please look at _____.

8. When <u>we</u> are late, out teacher gets angry at _____.

9. <u>My friends</u> sometimes write to me, and I sometimes write to _____.

10. <u>I</u> talk to her, and she talks to _____.

11. <u>We</u> help them, and they help _____.

12. <u>My outfit</u> is new. Do you like _____?

13. <u>Her shoes</u> are comfortable. Do you like _____?

14. <u>She</u> is our English teacher. We like _____ a lot.

15. <u>Francisco</u> is my best friend. I like being with _____.

16. <u>This CD</u> is great. Do you like _____?

EXERCISE 6 Two friends are talking on the phone. Fill in each blank with the appropriate object pronoun.

Example: How often do you write to *them* _____?

A: I like Miami, but I miss my parents.

B: How often do you see (1) _____?

A: About twice a year. They often call (2) _____, and sometimes I send (3) _____ e-mails.

B: How about your sister Joanne? Do you talk with (4) _____ much?

A: Not much. I miss (5) _____ a lot.

B: Does she come to visit (6) _____?

A: No. She wants to, but hotels are too expensive, and my apartment is too small.

Grammar Focus

Use with student text page 130.

Recognize and Use Comparative Adjectives

	SIMPLE	COMPARATIVE
One-syllable adjectives and adverbs	tall	taller
	fast	faster
	sad	sadder
	big	bigger
Two-syllable adjectives that end in –*y*	easy	easier
	happy	happier
(Note spelling changes in words ending in –*y.*)		
Other two-syllable adjectives	frequent	more frequent
	active	more active
Some two-syllable adjectives have two forms	simple	simpler
		more simple
(Other two-syllable adjectives that have two forms are *handsome, quiet, gentle, narrow, clever, common, friendly, angry, polite, stupid.*)		
Adjectives with three or more syllables	important	more important
	difficult	more difficult
–*ly* adverbs	quickly	more quickly
Irregular adjectives / adverbs	good / well	better
	bad / badly	worse
	far	farther
	little	less
	a lot	more

LANGUAGE NOTE:
Bored and *tired* are considered two-syllable adjectives and use *more* in the comparative form.
    I am *more tired* than you today.
    I am *the most tired* of our whole team.

EXERCISE 1 Fill in the missing simple or comparative adjective.

Example: cold _____*colder*_____

1. good _____
2. fast _____
3. polite _____
4. _____ worse
5. busy _____
6. quiet _____
7. intelligent _____
8. _____ lazier
9. _____ friendlier
10. famous _____
11. ugly _____
12. _____ older

EXERCISE 2 Some students are talking about the food at school. Write the comparative form of the adjective.

Example: (delicious) The spaghetti is _____*more delicious*_____ than the tacos.

1. (expensive) Roast beef is _____ than hot dogs.
2. (cheap) The potato chips are _____ than the French fries.
3. (fresh) The salad is _____ than the fruit cup.
4. (large) The cheeseburger is _____ than the hamburger.
5. (good) The food is _____ at lunch than at dinner.
6. (nice) The tables outside are _____ than the tables inside.
7. (big) The juices in the cafeteria are _____ than the juices from the vending machine.
8. (polite) The servers here are _____ than the servers at my other school.
9. (sweet) This candy is _____ than that candy.
10. (bad) This cafeteria is terrible. The pizza is _____ than the spaghetti.
11. (small) The portions are _____ at lunch than at dinner.
12. (hot) The soup in the cafeteria is _____ than the soup from the lunch truck.

Name _____ Date _____

Write the appropriate comparative adjective on the line.

Example: Kile is (smart) than Margaux.   _smarter_

1. Margaux works (hard) than Kile.   _____
2. Kile is a (lazy) student than Margaux.   _____
3. Ben is (intelligent) than Kile.   _____
4. Margaux is (friendly) than Kile and Ben.   _____
5. Reading is (easy) for Ben than it is for Kile.   _____
6. Jeffrey is (popular) than Ben.   _____
7. Ben is (happy) than Jeffrey.   _____
8. Margaux is (energetic) than Ben.   _____

EXERCISE 4 Rewrite each sentence using the correct form of the comparative adjective.

Example: People often compare twins to see who is tallerer.
People often compare twins to see who is taller.

1. Sometimes, people think that one twin has a betterer personality than the other one.

   _____

2. They also compare them to see who is more smarterer.

   _____

3. People think that one twin might be more funnerer than the other twin.

   _____

4. People also think that one twin might be more artisticer than the other twin.

   _____

5. They think that one twin might even be more athleticer than the other twin.

   _____

6. Twins might agree that one of them is a more fast runner than the other.

   _____

7. They might also agree that one of them eats more healthier than the other.

   _____

8. Mostly, each of them knows that being their own person is importanter than comparing themselves to each other.

   _____

EXERCISE 5 Rewrite each sentence using the comparative form of the adjective in parentheses.

Example: Yesterday was (hot) than Monday. *Yesterday was hotter than Monday.*

1. This summer has been (warm) than last summer.

    _____

2. This time last summer, it was (cool) by at least five degrees.

    _____

3. This summer seems (sunny) than last summer.

    _____

4. Last summer was (rainy) than this summer.

    _____

5. The warm weather has helped the flowers bloom (early) than last summer.

    _____

6. This summer, we had to water the flowers and shrubs (often) than last summer.

    _____

7. It is hard to say if the flowers are (beautiful) this year than they were last year.

    _____

8. Colorful flowers are (pretty) than wilted ones.

    _____

9. Sunshine and flowers make people (happy) than ice and snow.

    _____

10. The temperature this time next summer may be (mild) than it has been this summer.

    _____

Grammar Focus

Identify the Subject and Verb of a Sentence

EXAMPLE	EXPLANATION
S V The flowers bloomed. S V The woman purchased new shoes.	The subject (S) comes before the verb (V).
S S V The teachers and students saw the school play. S V V We cooked and ate our lunch.	There can be more than one subject (S) in a sentence. There can be more than one verb (V) in a sentence.

LANGUAGE NOTES:

1. The subject of a sentence is the word or phrase that performs the action.
2. The verb is the action performed by the subject.
3. There can be more than one subject or verb in a sentence.

EXERCISE 1   Fill in each blank with the subject.

Example: Restaurants serve food.   *Restaurants*

1. Chefs and waitresses work in restaurants. _____
2. The maitre d' takes reservations and seats customers. _____
3. Upon arrival, customers walk to their table and receive a menu. _____
4. A menu outlines the dishes that are available. _____
5. Salad is a popular appetizer. _____
6. Pasta and vegetables come with some meals. _____
7. Chicken and steak are popular dinner entrees. _____
8. The evening's specials appear on the menu. _____
9. Many people consider dessert the best part of the meal. _____
10. Fruit salad is a healthy dessert. _____
11. Chocolate cake and chocolate ice cream taste delicious. _____
12. My friend orders and eats dessert at every restaurant. _____
13. We always split the check. _____
14. Sometimes, my friend and I wrap and take home leftovers. _____

Name _____ Date _____

EXERCISE 2 Circle the subject and underline the verb in each sentence.

Example: (Summer) attracts people to the beach.

1. Some people travel hours to the beach.

2. They love the sun, sand, and surf.

3. The beach is a great place on a hot day.

4. The water feels cool and refreshing.

5. Lifeguards post warnings about the swimming conditions.

6. The signs say different things.

7. The waves are rough.

8. The currents are strong.

9. Lifeguards protect people from danger.

10. Lifeguards teach people beach safety.

EXERCISE 3 Fill in the blank with a subject to complete each sentence.

Example: The _dog_ barked loudly.

1. The _____ purred.

2. The _____ roared.

3. The _____ is a place where you go to visit animals.

4. _____ is the first and most important meal of the day.

5. A _____ is a place that has books you can borrow.

6. A _____ is a place where you buy groceries.

7. A _____ keeps your head warm when it is cold outside.

8. An _____ is a place where you go to catch an airplane.

9. A _____ is a room in your house where you cook dinner.

10. A _____ is a professional who is trained to help you get better when you feel sick.

Name _____   Date _____

EXERCISE 4 Write *S* and *V* over the subjects and verbs in each sentence.

                 S   V

Example: Tim leads a healthy lifestyle.

1. Tim exercises every day.

2. He runs three miles in the morning.

3. After school, he works out at the gym.

4. He eats and drinks foods and beverages full of vitamins.

5. Fruits and vegetables are a large part of his diet.

6. Exercise and a healthy diet keep Tim fit and make him feel good.

7. Tim convinces his friend Jerry to exercise, too.

8. Jerry runs with Tim in the morning.

9. Jerry told Tim that he looks and feels better than he ever has.

10. Tim agreed and suggested that it's because of all that exercise.

EXERCISE 5 Fill in the blank with a verb to complete each sentence.

Example: Johnny _likes_ baseball.

1. He _____ to games whenever he can.
2. He _____ the team his friend likes.
3. Last week, his team _____ against his friend's favorite team.
4. His team _____.
5. He _____ happy.
6. His friend _____ upset.
7. They _____ not to talk about it.
8. They _____ to go to a movie next time.

Name _____ Date _____

EXERCISE 6 Write *S* or *V* over the subjects and verbs in each sentence.

            S   V

Example: Kimberly is a fair person.

1. Kimberly never judges anyone.

2. She works as an office manager.

3. Her job requires a lot of patience.

4. She meets and greets new people all the time.

5. She talks to them and addresses their questions.

6. She also answers phones and distributes important forms.

7. People in her office ask her for help all the time.

8. She listens to their problems and finds solutions.

9. Her friends and colleagues consider her a kind person.

10. Kimberly always wins and keeps the respect of every person she meets.

EXERCISE 7 Circle the subjects and underline the verbs in this paragraph.

Example: (America) <u>is</u> a big country.

America has oceans, lakes, rivers, mountains, and valleys. America features fifty states. The United States contains 48 of the 50 states. Alaska and Hawaii are located many miles from the other states. Each state offers something unique. Some states experience four different seasons. Other states are warm several months of the year. Every state you visit thrills and delights.

43

Grammar Focus

Talk About the Future Using *Will* and *Shall*

SUBJECT	*WILL*	(*NOT*)	VERB	COMPLEMENT
I	will		buy	a gift.
She	will	not	give	money.
There	will		be	250 people at the wedding.

LANGUAGE NOTES:

1. Use *will* with all persons to form the future tense. *Will* doesn't have an *–s* form.
2. A contraction can be formed with a subject pronoun and *will:* *I'll, you'll, he'll, she'll, it'll, we'll,* and *they'll.*
3. Put *not* after *will* to form the negative. The contraction for *will not* is *won't. Will not* is very strong and formal. *Won't* is used often in informal conversation.
4. A frequency word can go between *will* and the main verb: She will *never* understand American customs.
5. We can form a question with *will* and *won't.*
   Will he stay?
   Won't you join us?
   When *will* she arrive?
   Why *won't* they leave?

EXERCISE 1 Unscramble the words to form sentences.

Example: it / today / sunny / be / will *It will be sunny today.*

1. doctor / I / become / will / a _____
2. you / will / in / Germany / live _____
3. soon / get / will / a new job / he _____
4. she / will / leave / never _____
5. will / write / a book / they _____
6. together / tomorrow / will / play / the girls _____
7. have / a wonderful time / we / will _____
8. not / will / rain / it / this weekend _____
9. a party / will / be / there / not _____
10. will / never / I / promise / that _____

EXERCISE 2 Fill in each blank with an appropriate verb in the future tense. Use *will* or *won't*.

I (**Example:** have) ___will have___ a very busy summer. First, my family

(1: come) _____ to visit me in the city. We (2: go) _____ to museums and

to many nice stores. My brother (3: see) _____ all the big summer movies. My father

and mother (4: not / go) _____ to the movies. My sister (5: spend) _____

all of her money on shoes. My mother and father (6: not / spend) _____ money on

clothes. They (7: want) _____ to eat in nice restaurants.

After three days, we (8: travel) _____ to the shore. My family

(9: stay) _____ there for one week. We (10: take) _____ a picnic lunch to

the beach every day. My brother and sister (11: swim) _____ all day. I

(12: play) _____ volleyball with my friends. This (13: be) _____ a

great summer! I hope you (14: come) _____ with us.

EXERCISE 3 Rewrite each sentence below in the future tense with *will*. Some sentences are negative.

Example: He eats a sandwich. _He will eat a sandwich._

She doesn't drink soda. _She will not drink soda./She won't drink soda._

1. Jessica goes to school. _____
2. My mother drives her car. _____
3. Hank needs a hammer. _____
4. They do not eat cake. _____
5. Paula walks to work. _____
6. Arthur studies Spanish. _____
7. Ken buys a plant. _____
8. The trees are in bloom. _____
9. Mina isn't happy. _____
10. I don't wear glasses. _____
11. You have good grades. _____
12. They fly home on holidays. _____
13. I don't wash the dishes. _____
14. We are happy. _____
15. My sister has a baby boy. _____

Name _____ Date _____

EXERCISE 4 Use the contraction of *will* ('*ll*) with the subject pronouns or *will not* (*won't*) to complete each statement.

Example: (I / not / get on) _____*I won't get on*_____ the bus at 7:30 A.M.

1. (I / call) _____ you when I arrive in the city.
2. (He / not / be) _____ at the bus station.
3. (You / not / need) _____ any money for the taxi.
4. (You / buy) _____ a house one day.
5. (She / meet) _____ you on the street corner.
6. (They / not / like) _____ the menu in the cafeteria.
7. (We / not / go) _____ if it rains tomorrow.
8. (It / be) _____ cloudy in the morning.
9. (It / not / rain) _____ I'm sure.
10. (I / walk) Tomorrow _____ 5 miles.
11. (she / not / play) Tonight _____ basketball.
12. (I / not / look) _____ at my birthday present yet.
13. (He / be) _____ ready for the game.
14. (We / listen) _____ to the music at the concert.

EXERCISE 5 Write questions using *will* and the words in parentheses.

Example: (Why / you / not / be) _____*Why won't you be*_____ there tomorrow?

1. (Where / you / go) _____ to college?
2. (How long / they / study) _____ English?
3. (Why / she / not / finish) _____ that book?
4. (Whom / he / go) _____ to the concert with?
5. (When / we / see) _____ you and your family?
6. (What / you / do) _____ this weekend?
7. (Why / not / you / eat) _____ the fish?
8. (How long / he / try) _____ to get that job?
9. (Where / she / keep) _____ her new dog?
10. (Where / it / be) _____ nice to visit?

VISIONS A Grammar Practice • Copyright © Thomson Heinle

Name _____ Date _____

EXERCISE 6 Finish each sentence or question in this conversation using *will* or *won't* plus the verb in parentheses. Use contractions when possible.

Example: **Jane:** [I see] _____*I'll see*_____ you when I return to school.

Jane: Hi, John! When [(1) I meet] _____ your family?

John: Sorry, Jane. My family [(2) not / be] _____ here this week. We

[(3) not /stay] _____ in the city during our school break. We

[(4) rent] _____ a small cabin on a lake for one week. What

[(5) you do] _____ during the school break?

Jane: I think [(6) travel] _____ a little. [(7) I not /go] _____ home.

My friends and I [(8) try] _____ to rent a car.

John: [(9) be] _____ the car rental _____ expensive?

Jane: I don't think so. We [(10) share] _____ the cost.

John: It sounds like [(11) you have] _____ a great time.

Jane: I hope so. I know [(12) I miss] _____ my family.

John: Have a safe trip, Jane!

EXERCISE 7 Use the words to make future statements with *will*. Use contractions when possible.

Example: I / move / to the city / in July *I'll move to the city in July.*

1. Emir / change (negative) / his study habits

_____

2. Juan / start / college / in the fall

_____

3. I / participate / more / in class

_____

4. they / return (negative) / to Poland / next year

_____

5. I / forget (negative) / my classmates

_____

6. my family / come / to my graduation / in June

_____

Grammar Focus

Use with student text page 174.

Use Verbs with Infinitives

SUBJECT	VERB	INFINITIVE	COMPLEMENT
I	want	**to get**	the best price.
The salesperson	hopes	**to make**	a sale.
We	are planning	**to buy**	a new TV.

LANGUAGE NOTES:

1. An infinitive is *to* + the base form of a verb.
2. We can use an infinitive after the following verbs:

agree	forget	prefer
ask	hope	promise
attempt	learn	refuse
begin	like	remember
continue	love	start
decide	need	try
expect	plan	want

3. An infinitive never has an ending. It never shows the tense. Only the first verb shows the tense.

EXERCISE 1   Circle each infinitive.

Example: I love (to try) on new clothes.

1.   I begin to think about that show.

2.   The teacher tries to explain the grammar.

3.   The children promise to be good.

4.   The doctor needs to see the patients.

5.   You like to have new adventures, don't you?

6.   I expect to see your family someday soon.

7.   They continue to love their baseball team.

8.   She started to get a head cold.

9.   My mother prefers to drink herbal tea.

10.   We all want to go on a vacation.

Name _____ Date _____

Fill in each blank with the infinitive form of a verb from the box.

invade	receive	wait	help	be	destroy
work	send	lose	resist	give	

Example: The soldiers tried _____to invade_____ the city, but they couldn't.

1. No one expected the city _____ able to resist their attack.
2. The government hoped _____ more soldiers to defend the city.
3. The enemy forgot _____ the main bridge across the river.
4. The government asked other countries _____.
5. The other countries preferred _____ and see what happened.
6. They promised _____ whatever aid they could.
7. The people didn't want _____ their homes to the enemy.
8. They learned _____ together for the common good.
9. They continued _____ the enemy month after month.
10. They needed _____ fresh supplies of food and arms.

Circle the infinitives. Then choose an appropriate verb for each blank. The verbs in the box below may be used more than one time each. Use the correct verb tense.

decide	hope	prefer
continue	refuse	like
ask	promise	want
need	begin	start

Example: At a wedding last week, the bride and groom ____promised____ (to love) each other.

1. After much discussion, we _____ to talk about the pollution problem.
2. It _____ to rain day after day after day.
3. My parents _____ to retire while they are still healthy and active.
4. The policeman _____ to see the woman's driver's license.
5. She _____ to show it to him.
6. You _____ to tell me what kind of flowers you wanted me to buy.
7. You _____ to write it down.
8. They _____ to take their vacation in the winter.
9. Daddy opened the book and _____ to read to us.
10. It's getting dark in here. We _____ to turn on some lights.

EXERCISE 4 Unscramble the words. Then give a short answer with information about yourself.

Example: want / buy / new car / to / do / you
Do you want to buy a new car?   *No, I don't.*

1. like / sweets / you / eat / to / do

   _____   _____

2. try / you / exercise / every day / to / do

   _____   _____

3. do / want / on a vacation / go / you / to

   _____   _____

4. to / you / do / plan / go to college

   _____   _____

5. expect / use / English / in the future / to / do / you

   _____   _____

EXERCISE 5 Make a sentence with the words given.

Example: I / like / play *I like to play the Spanish guitar.* _____

1. I / like / listen to _____
2. she / love / go _____
3. he / try / learn _____
4. you / want / buy _____
5. we / need / find _____
6. I / hope / finish _____
7. they / continue / practice _____
8. I / try / think _____
9. we / begin / like _____
10. you / not / prefer / eat _____
11. my friend / want / try _____
12. he / decide / learn _____

VISIONS A Grammar Practice • Copyright © Thomson Heinle

Name _____ Date _____

EXERCISE 6 Unscramble the words to make correct sentences.

Example: want / they / me / sign / some papers / to *They want me to sign some papers.*

1. need / they / write / a check / me / to _____
2. see / plan / I / them / this afternoon / to _____
3. expect / arrive / them / I / at 1:00 / to _____
4. see / hope / them sooner / I / to _____
5. wait / expect / they / me / for them / to _____
6. need / do some shopping / I / to _____
7. will / finish early / try / I / to _____
8. won't / meet them / I / forget / to _____

EXERCISE 7 Complete each sentence using a verb from each box.

ask	begin	try	~~learn~~	expect	agree	decide	want	plan
open	eat	give	~~use~~	let	have	arrive	sit	leave

Example: I ___*learned*___ ___*to use*___ the ATM yesterday.

1. I _____ _____ a savings account in a week or two.
2. The teller _____ _____ me 200 checks when I asked a second time.
3. The customers _____ _____ at 9:00 this morning.
4. The teller _____ the bank _____ a busy day.
5. She was tired, so she _____ _____ down.
6. She _____ _____ lunch at noon, but she couldn't.
7. She _____ _____, but the boss wouldn't let her go.
8. She _____ him _____ her go, but he said no.

EXERCISE 8 Unscramble the words to write sentences with infinitives.

Example: wants / to / Raquel / go / shopping   *Raquel wants to go shopping.*

1. buy / a new dress / she / needs / to   _____
2. shopping / Marie / go / loves / to / too   _____
3. they / this / are / to / go / trying / afternoon   _____
4. new clothes / I / buy / don't / to / need   _____

51

Grammar Focus

Use with student text page 188.

Use Compound Sentences With *and*

COMPLETE SENTENCE		COMPLETE SENTENCE	
SUBJECT		**SUBJECT**	
The house	<u>is</u> in a quiet neighborhood.	**The house**	<u>has</u> a swimming pool.
The house	<u>is</u> in a quiet neighborhood, **and**	**it**	<u>has</u> a swimming pool.
The house is in a quiet neighborhood, and it has a swimming pool.			
The rooms	<u>have</u> air conditioning.	**The rooms**	<u>are</u> in good condition.
The rooms	<u>have</u> air conditioning, **and**	**they**	<u>are</u> in good condition.
The rooms have air conditioning, and they are in good condition.			

LANGUAGE NOTES:

1. Two complete sentences can be combined using a conjunction. A comma appears before the conjunction.
2. Conjunctions include: *and, but,* and *so.*
3. The conjunction *and* joins together related ideas.
   The book was popular, *and* it was on sale at the local bookstore.
4. The conjunction *but* joins together contrasting ideas.
   Liam wanted to play outside, *but* it was raining.
5. The conjunction *so* shows the result of a consequence.
   She had a lot of homework to do, *so* she started as soon as she got home.
   So can also mean "in order that."
   I stayed, *so* I could see you.

EXERCISE 1 Underline the two parts of each sentence. Make sure to put a comma before the conjunction.

Example: <u>My apartment has five rooms</u>, and <u>it has a beautiful view from the balcony.</u>

1. The rent is $800 a month and the utilities are included.
2. The living room has a fireplace and the kitchen is large.
3. Nikolai and Andrea need an apartment and they are looking in the classified ads.
4. His mom wants an apartment with three bedrooms and they need a washer/dryer.
5. Our dream house is in a friendly neighborhood and it has a swimming pool.
6. Peter and I are buying a house in September and we need new furniture.

Name _____ Date _____

EXERCISE 2 Fill in each blank with the correct conjunction.

Example: Conjunctions help you combine sentences, _so_ conjunctions are important.

Two sentences can be combined using a conjunction, (1) _____ a comma must always follow the conjunction. Several words are joining words, (2) _____ they include *and*, *but*, and *so*.

Authors often want to make their writing interesting, (3) _____ they use conjunctions to combine two complete sentences. They use simple sentences, (4) _____ compound sentences add variety to their work.

EXERCISE 3 Combine the two sentences using *and*, *but*, or *so*. Make sure to put a comma before the conjunction.

Example: Seth needs a new computer. He plans to buy one.
Seth needs a new computer, and he plans to buy one.

1. Seth asked his friend which computer to purchase. His friend recommended the Starpac 3000.
   _____

2. Seth called the local computer store. He asked to speak with a sales associate.
   _____

3. There were no available associates. He drove to the store.
   _____

4. He arrived at the store. He was unable to find the Starpac 3000.
   _____

5. He surveyed the selection of computers. He didn't like anything else he saw.
   _____

6. He decided to try another computer store. He started to make his way to the door.
   _____

7. He was about to leave. A sales associate stopped him.
   _____

8. The associate asked Seth if he needed any help. Seth said that he did.
   _____

9. Seth explained to the associate that he was interested in the Starpac 3000. The associate led him right to it.
   _____

10. The associate answered all of Seth's questions. Seth wasn't sure if he wanted the Starpac 3000 after all.

_____

11. The associate said that the Starpac 3000 was the best computer on the market. It was on sale for a limited time.

_____

12. Seth decided he would buy it. The associate brought Seth's new computer to the front of the store.

_____

13. Seth made his purchase. He has been very happy ever since he brought home his new computer.

_____

14. Seth thanked his friend for the recommendation. He invited his friend to see the new computer.

_____

EXERCISE 4 Underline the two parts of each sentence. Then fill in each blank with the correct conjunction.

Example: _The bus waited to take the students to the museum, so it was parked outside the school._

1. The students in Mrs. Staria's class brought their permission slips to school, _____ Mrs. Staria collected them.

2. The students were supposed to submit their permission slips, _____ three of them left them at home.

3. The students apologized to Mrs. Staria for neglecting to bring their completed permission slips to school, _____ Mrs. Staria told them that it was no problem.

4. Mrs. Staria called each of their parents, _____ they were not home.

5. Mrs. Staria called each of their parents at work, _____ she was able to get permission for them to go to the museum.

6. Mrs. Staria told her students it was time to leave, _____ the students began to walk toward the bus.

7. The bus driver opened the door, _____ the students began filing onto the bus.

8. The bus arrived at the museum twenty minutes early, _____ the museum was not open.

9. The students were excited, _____ they waited patiently for the museum to open.

10. The clock struck 9:00, _____ the excited students exited the bus and headed for the museum.

11. The students listened carefully to the curator, _____ they asked her a lot of very good questions.

12. A few of the students wanted to know how they could become curators, _____ the curator explained that there are graduate programs available.

13. One student wasn't sure he could remember all the things he would have to know, _____ the curator reassured him.

VISIONS A Grammar Practice • Copyright © Thomson Heinle

14. The students' visit to the museum ended, _____ they didn't want to leave.

15. The curator said that she was glad they enjoyed their visit, _____ she encouraged them to come back to the museum soon.

EXERCISE 5 Combine the two sentences using *and, but,* or *so*. Make sure to put a comma before the conjunction.

Example: The library is an important resource. Mr. Steuben, the school librarian, shows students what the library has to offer.

The library is an important resource, so Mr. Steuben, the school librarian,

shows students what the library has to offer.

1. Mr. Garretson wanted his students to learn about the library's resources. He scheduled a tour of the library for them.

   _____

2. Mr. Garretson's class entered the library. They were greeted by Mr. Steuben, the school librarian.

   _____

3. The students looked around. Some of them didn't understand why they were there.

   _____

4. Mr. Garretson asked the students if there was something they were curious about. No one could think of anything.

   _____

5. Mr. Garretson wanted to engage the students. He asked them if they ever wondered when cellular phones were invented.

   _____

6. The students nodded excitedly. Mr. Steuben began his introduction.

   _____

7. He showed them the how to conduct a card catalog search on the computer. He showed them how to find the books from the search.

   _____

8. The students learned how to locate books. They learned how to locate magazines and journals, too.

   _____

9. Mr. Steuben's tour of the library proved fun and informative. Every student left the library with a book and a new understanding.

   _____

10. For weeks, Mr. Garretson's students have talked about their trip to the library. Many of them have returned to the library several times since the tour.

   _____

Grammar Focus

Use with student text page 204.

Use *Could and Couldn't*

MODAL	ALTERNATE EXPRESSION	EXPLANATION
She **can** pay up to $300 for her plane ticket.	**It is possible** for her to pay up to $300 for her plane ticket.	Possibility
I **can't** get the door to open. I **can** speak three languages.	We **are not able to** get the door to open.	Ability
We **can't** take more than two bags onto the plane.	We **are not allowed to / are not permitted to** take more than two bags onto the plane.	Permission
You **may** leave whenever you want to.	You **are allowed to / are permitted** to leave whenever you want to.	Permission
I **couldn't** operate a computer three years ago, but I **can** now.	I **wasn't able to** operate a computer three years ago, but I **am able to** now.	Past ability
I **couldn't** drive until I got a license, but now I **can.**	I **wasn't permitted to** drive until I got a license, but now I **am permitted to / am allowed to.**	Past permission

LANGUAGE NOTES:

1. *Can, could, may, might,* and *should* are modals. Modals are verbs that show possibility, ability, and permission.
2. *Could* is the past form of *can.*
   I couldn't *see the show last week, but I can see it now.*
3. *Could* and *might* show there is a chance that something will happen in the future.
   You could *have had an accident.*
   You might *get hurt.*
4. *May* shows that permission is being given.
   You may *help yourself to some dessert.*
5. *Should* refers to something that is expected.
   You should *have canceled your appointment.*
   The negative form of could *and* should *are* couldn't *and* shouldn't.

VISIONS A Grammar Practice • Copyright © Thomson Heinle

EXERCISE 1 Underline each modal or modal expression and write an alternative expression in its place.

Example: I <u>can't</u> pay $1,200 a year for car insurance.

It isn't possible for me to pay $1,200 a year for car insurance.

1. My sister can babysit on Saturday nights.

_____

2. Don can play the guitar and the piano.

_____

3. Nancy can use Ed's van this weekend.

_____

4. The children may watch TV until 9:00 P.M.

_____

5. I could sing very well when I was young, but now I can't.

_____

6. We could drive without seatbelts two years ago, but now we can't.

_____

7. It isn't possible for me to take a vacation soon.

_____

8. The little boy wasn't allowed to stay up late last year, but now he is.

_____

9. The runner wasn't able to cut time off his speed this year.

_____

10. She isn't able to pay her rent on time every month.

_____

11. He isn't permitted to plan the parade.

_____

12. The students are allowed to take the test home.

_____

EXERCISE 2 Underline each modal or modal expression and change it to the negative past tense.

Example: He <u>can</u> pay the credit card bill today.

(last week) *He couldn't pay the credit card bill last week.*

1. Amy can play the flute very well this year.

    (last year) _____

2. Janet is allowed to take out books from the library this week.

    (last week) _____

3. We are able to play soccer as a team this month.

    (two months ago) _____

4. It is possible for Eric to earn a lot of money in this job.

    (in his previous job) _____

5. Lily can pronounce English very well this semester.

    (last semester) _____

6. They may live in the dormitories this term.

    (last term) _____

EXERCISE 3 Fill in each blank with *could*, *might*, or *should*.

Example: It's good to have disability insurance. You _____*could*_____ get sick.

1. If you want my advice, you _____ take the new job.
2. All full-time employees _____ work at least 35 hours a week.
3. I'm not sure, but I _____ get a raise next month.
4. If you want to, you _____ ask for a day off.
5. All part-time employees _____ work less than 20 hours a week.
6. You _____ be nicer to the boss if you want a raise.
7. You _____ get a raise if you're nicer to her.
8. The U.S. government _____ give everyone free health insurance.

EXERCISE 4 Complete each sentence with *could, might,* or *should*. Then write *a, b, c,* or *d* in the blank to show how the modal is used.

    a. to show there is a chance something will happen

    b. to give advice

    c. to show there is one correct way to do something

    d. to show that something is necessary

Example: _b_ You <u>should</u> do your homework every night.

1. _____ Don't smoke in the storeroom. It _____ start a fire.

2. _____ You _____ take shorter breaks.

3. _____ The smaller boxes _____ go on top of the bigger boxes.

4. _____ Everyone _____ pay taxes.

5. _____ You _____ get good grades if you study hard.

6. _____ You _____ arrive on time if you don't want to get in trouble.

7. _____ You _____ wear shoes to school.

8. _____ The manager _____ pay me $14 an hour. It's in my contract.

9. _____ They _____ open another school down the street.

10. _____ You've worked hard. You _____ ask for a bonus.

EXERCISE 5 Underline each modal. Then write each sentence in the negative past tense.

Example: I <u>should</u> find a job for the summer.

                    I *shouldn't* find a job for the summer.

1. I could look through the job section of the newspaper.

    _____

2. I should work for myself.

    _____

3. I could start my own summer business.

    _____

4. I could mow the neighbors' lawns.

    _____

5. I should charge a fee for my services.

    _____

Grammar Focus

Use with student text page 220.

Recognize Complex Sentences with *If*

EXAMPLE	EXPLANATION
If we study hard, we will pass the test.	Use *if* to show that the condition affects the result.
Even if we study tonight, we might not pass the test.	Use *even if* to show that the condition doesn't affect the result.
Unless we study, we won't pass the test.	Use *unless* to mean *if . . . not* or *except if*.

LANGUAGE NOTES:

1. Complex sentences are made up of an independent clause and a dependent clause. An independent clause can stand on its own. A dependent clause cannot stand on its own.

    Dependent   Independent

    Clause   Clause

    If I get an invitation, I will go to the wedding.

2. In a future sentence, use the simple present tense in the condition clause.

    If my brother *comes* to school here, he *will live* with me.

EXERCISE 1 Underline the dependent clause. Circle the independent clause.

Example: (He will ruin his health) if he keeps smoking cigarettes.

1. If she doesn't stop working so many hours, she will get sick.

2. She will not graduate if she doesn't start studying harder.

3. If she pays attention to her work, she will pass the test.

4. You can't learn to speak a foreign language if you don't practice.

5. You shouldn't try to learn a language if you don't have enough time to devote to it.

6. If you are patient and practice a lot, you will learn the language you are studying.

EXERCISE 2 Complete each statement.

Example: You shouldn't eat your dessert if *you don't eat your vegetables.*

1. You can't go abroad if _____

2. You can't enter this school unless _____

3. Students can't go to the next level if _____

4. You can't borrow books from the library if _____

5. Students aren't allowed to miss class unless _____

6. You shouldn't talk in class unless _____

7. Students aren't allowed to eat in class unless _____

8. Students usually eat at the cafeteria unless _____

9. You shouldn't leave school early unless _____

10. Students are expected to do their homework even if _____

EXERCISE 3 Fill in each blank with *if, even if,* or *unless.*

Example: _____*If*_____ a person eats fruit and vegetables, he or she will probably live longer.

1. _____ people eat healthy food, they may get sick.

2. _____ children learn about good health at an early age, they might develop poor health habits.

3. _____ researchers are getting closer to finding a cure for cancer, many people die of it each year.

4. _____ we solve some of our environmental problems, more and more people will get cancer.

5. _____ people want to live longer, they must be willing to take steps toward developing a healthier lifestyle.

6. _____ you lead a healthy lifestyle, there is no guarantee you will live a long life.

7. _____ people are aware of health hazards in the environment, they cannot take precautions.

8. _____ people realized how dangerous the sun can be, they would not lie in the sun for hours.

9. _____ you wear sun protection, you can be severely burned.

10. Your skin will be healthy longer _____ you cover it at the beach.

EXERCISE 4 Complete each statement.

Example: If I don't eat dinner, *I'm going to feel hungry.*_____

1. If I don't come to school, _____

2. If I study every day, _____

3. If I don't study every day, _____

4. If I make a lot of money, _____

EXERCISE 5 Correct the error in each sentence.

                                                            eats

Example: She will develop diabetes if she ~~will eats~~ too much sugar.

1. If Ali becomes a dentist, he makes a lot of money.

2. Paulo will hurt his ankle if he will run too far.

3. Peter will gain weight if he will eat large servings of food at every meal.

4. If you will be an obstetrician, you will work with mothers and babies.

5. If you exercise every day, it benefits your circulatory system.

6. If you will be in a good mood, your blood pressure won't be too high.

7. If you visit the dentist, she checks your teeth.

8. You will be healthy if you will eat enough fiber.

EXERCISE 6 Underline the dependent clauses. Circle the independent clauses.

Example: <u>If Bob forgets to set his alarm,</u> (he will oversleep.)

1. Bob will set his alarm if he doesn't want to oversleep.

2. If Bob oversleeps, he will miss his bus.

3. Bob will not miss the bus if he sets his alarm.

4. If Bob misses the bus, he will be late for school.

5. Bob will not be late for school if he catches the bus on time.

6. If Bob is late for school, he will be sent to the principal's office.

7. Bob will not be sent to the principal's office if he arrives at school on time.

8. If he is sent to the principal's office, he will have to stay after school.

9. Bob will be able to go home right after school if he gets to school on time.

10. If Bob goes home right after school, he will begin his homework.

11. Bob will finish his homework early if he begins it as soon as he gets home.

12. If Bob finishes his homework, he will be able to meet his friends at the park.

13. Bob will be able to play basketball with his friends if he meets them at the park.

EXERCISE 7 Fill in each blank with the correct tense of the verb in parentheses.

Example: If you (see) _see_ a psychiatrist, he (ask) _will ask_ why you are unhappy.

1. You (see) _____ a lot of children if you (become) _____ a pediatrician.
2. If you (run) _____ every day, you (develop) _____ endurance.
3. You (lower) _____ your blood pressure if you (exercise) _____ regularly.
4. You (increase) _____ the flexibility of your joints if you (stretch) _____ .
5. If you (see) _____ the dermatologist, he (look) _____ at your rash.
6. You (have) _____ difficulty running if you (have) _____ asthma.
7. If you (have) _____ a stroke, you (need) _____ to go to the hospital.
8. You (get) _____ an ulcer if you (worry) _____ too much.

EXERCISE 8 Fill in each blank with the correct tense of the verb in parentheses.

Example: Gary (go) _will go_ to the game if Andrea (go) _goes_ with him.

1. Gary and Andrea (walk) _____ to the game if the weather (cooperate) _____ .
2. If it (rain) _____ , they (drive) _____ .
3. They (wear) _____ baseball hats if the sun (shine) _____ too brightly.
4. If they (feel) _____ tired, they (stay) _____ home.
5. Gary and Andrea (buy) _____ tickets for the next home game if the team (wins) _____ .
6. If the team (lose) _____ , Gary and Andrea (watch) _____ the next home game on television.
7. They (exchange) _____ their tickets for another game if the game (be) _____ rained out.
8. If they (be) _____ hungry, they (purchase) _____ lunch at the game.

Name _____ Date _____

Grammar Focus

Use with student text page 240.

Use Prepositional Phrases

PREPOSITIONS			
The ball is **in** the box.		The ball is **between** two boxes.	
The ball is **on** the box.		The ball is **over** the box.	
The ball is **under** the box.		The ball is **in front of** the box.	
The ball is **next to** the box.		The ball is **behind** the box.	

LANGUAGE NOTES:

1. A prepositional phrase is a group of words that begins with a preposition and ends with a noun or pronoun.
   Patrick parked his car *across the street*.
   Alicia placed the book *on the table*.
2. Use prepositions to talk about where things are or when events occur.
3. Some other prepositions are: *about, across, across from after, around, at, behind, between, from, in, in front of, into, next to, on, over, through, to, toward, under,* and *until.*

EXERCISE 1 Complete each sentence with a preposition from the chart above. Then circle the prepositional phrase in each sentences.

Example: The clock is (over the desk). The desk is (_____*under*_____ the clock.)

1. The chair is behind the table. The table is _____ the chair.

2. The book is under the lamp. The lamp is _____ the book.

3. The sofa is under the painting. The painting is _____ the sofa.

4. The sofa is next to the lamp. The lamp is next to the table. The lamp is _____ the sofa and the table.

EXERCISE 2 Complete each sentence with the best preposition from the chart above.

				A	B
Example:	Where is Carmen? She is _____ the living room.	A. in	B. on	●	○
1.	Where is the clock? It's _____ the refrigerator.	A. in	B. over	○	○

2. Where is the telephone? It's _____ the TV and the computer.   A. between   B. over   ○   ○

3. Where is the trash can? It's _____ the table.   A. over   B. under   ○   ○

4. Where is the lamp? It's _____ the sofa.   A. between   B. next to   ○   ○

5. Where are the flowers? They are _____ the piano.   A. on   B. between   ○   ○

6. Where are the shoes? They are _____ the bed.   A. over   B. under   ○   ○

EXERCISE 3 Using *around, across, on, at, in,* or *from,* write the best preposition to complete each sentence.

Example: We like the gardens _____*in*_____ the park.

1. Do you like the bookstore _____ the mall?

2. My family lives _____ Mexico City.

3. The DMV is _____ Third Avenue.

4. Ty's not here. He is _____ school.

5. Do you live _____ a small town?

6. Please meet me _____ the park.

7. She lives _____ the corner from him.

8. They are _____ school today.

9. Is your school _____ the left?

10. _____ my house, go straight.

11. We work _____ 14 Maple Street.

12. I work _____ from the park.

EXERCISE 4 Match the sentence on the left with a picture on the right. Write the letter in the blank. Then, write *P* over the preposition in each sentences.

                                        P

Example: The square is *between* two circles. _____B_____   A.

1. The square goes to the *right.* _____   B.

2. The circle moves to the *left.* _____   C.

3. The circle is *on the corner.* _____   D.

4. The arrow goes *around the corner.* _____   E.

5. The square is *across from* the circle. _____   F.

EXERCISE 5 Complete the conversation. Use *in, on, at, next to,* and *across from.*

Example: Carlos: Is there an art museum (1) _____*in*_____ Centerville?

Steve: Sure. It's (2) _____ Elm Street.

Carlos: Is it (3) _____ the high school?

Steve: No, it's across the street from the high school. It's (4) _____ 450 Elm Street.

Carlos: Oh, I know. And is there a bus stop (5) _____ the art museum?

Steve: No, but there's one (6) _____ the corner of Elm Street and Center Street.

Carlos: I visited a great museum when I was (7) _____ England.

Steve: Is the museum (8) _____ London?

Carlos: Yes. It's called the Little Museum.

Steve: Is it next to the park (9) _____ Lester Street?

Carlos: No, it's (10) _____ the park.

Steve: Oh, that's right.

EXERCISE 6 Read each sentence. Number the places on the map. Then, underline the prepositional phrase in each sentence.

Example: There is a subway stop <u>at the corner</u> of Fifth Avenue and Main Street.

1. There is a Japanese restaurant across from the subway stop.

2. There is a hotel next to the Japanese restaurant.

3. There is a grocery store next to the bank.

4. There is an Italian restaurant across from the grocery store.

5. There is a furniture store across from the bank.

6. There is a pharmacy at the corner of Fifth Avenue and Center Street.

7. There is a department store on Center Street.

EXERCISE 7 Read the underlined phrase in each sentence. If it is a prepositional phrase, write *P*. If it is not, write *N*.

Example: Kate and Richetta spent the day <u>at the amusement park</u>.   *P*

1. Kate met Richetta <u>at the train station.</u>   _____

2. They purchased their tickets <u>at the ticket window.</u>   _____

3. They boarded <u>the train.</u>   _____

4. They handed their tickets <u>to the conductor.</u>   _____

5. They found two seats <u>across the aisle from each other.</u>   _____

6. The conductor walked <u>through the train car.</u>   _____

7. He collected <u>their train tickets.</u>   _____

8. They talked <u>about the rides at the amusement park.</u> _____

9. They decided <u>to try all the rides.</u> _____

10. Kate wanted <u>to try the Super Loop.</u> _____

11. Richetta headed <u>toward the Fabulous Flume.</u> _____

12. "I guess we're going <u>on the Fabulous Flume</u> first," said Kate. _____

13. "We can ride the Super Loop <u>after the Fabulous Flume</u>," replied Richetta. _____

14. Their journey <u>to the amusement park</u> was finally over. _____

15. They exited the train and headed <u>toward the park.</u> _____

EXERCISE **8** Put boxes around the prepositional phrase in each sentence and circle the preposition.

Example: Course registration took place ⓘⓝ the Smith Building .

1. Chesney took the bus to school.

2. He walked to the Smith Building.

3. The Smith Building is across from the student union.

4. It is also next to the library.

5. Chesney stood in front of the Smith Building.

6. He looked at the entrance to the building.

7. The excitement was written on his face.

8. He headed into the building.

9. He walked to Room 208 and got in line to register.

10. Chesney gave his registration form to Mrs. Donnelly.

11. Mrs. Donnelly looked at his form, stamped it, and directed him to Room 215.

12. Chesney said "thank you" to Mrs. Donnelly and took his form to Room 215.

13. Chesney gave his stamped form to Mr. Fontanelle.

14. Mr. Fontanelle pulled up Chesney's record on the computer.

15. "Congratulations!" Mr. Fontanelle said to Chesney. "You are officially registered as a Sophomore at Elm Street High School."

Grammar Focus

Use with student text page 250.

Identify Prepositional Phrases of Time

PREPOSITION	EXAMPLE

on: days and dates	When do you do laundry?
	     On Saturdays.
	 When do Canadian people celebrate New Year's Eve?
	     On December 31.

in: months	When do British people celebrate Christmas? *In* December.
in: years	When do Americans vote for a president? *In* 2000, 2004, 2008, and so on.
at: specific time of day	What time does the class start? *At* eight o'clock.

in: the morning
 in: the afternoon
 in: the evening
	When do you work?
	     In the afternoon.
	 When do you go to school?
	     In the morning.

at: night	When do you call your family? *At* night.
in: seasons	When do we have a vacation? *In* the summer.
from . . . to: a beginning and ending time	What hours do they work? *From* nine *to* five.

LANGUAGE NOTE:

A prepositional phrase is a group of words that begins with a preposition and ends with a noun or pronoun.

    Donna is going *in the morning.*

    Her appointment is *at 9:00* A.M.

EXERCISE 1 Circle the correct preposition to complete each sentence.

Example: I will graduate from college (in)/ on 2004.

1. People often go to church <u>at / on</u> Sunday.

2. My husband works <u>from / for</u> nine to six.

3. <u>On / In</u> the winter we read a lot of books.

4. I put the cat outside <u>on / at</u> night.

5. My mother's birthday is <u>on</u> / in April.

6. I want to buy a car <u>in</u> / at 2010.

7. <u>At</u> / In the morning, we walk for exercise.

8. The movie is <u>from</u> / at 7:30 to 9:30.

9. I go to bed <u>at</u> / from midnight.

10. My wedding anniversary is <u>in</u> / on August 17.

11. He likes to relax <u>on</u> / in the evening.

12. She enjoys long walks <u>in</u> / at the fall.

EXERCISE 2 Fill in each blank with the correct preposition. Place a box around the prepositional phrase.

Example: Palm City is a wonderful place to visit | __*in*__ the summer.|

1. The temperature is usually 80 degrees Fahrenheit _____ the afternoon.

2. _____ night, it is often about 70 degrees.

3. It was 85 degrees _____ July 30.

4. People in Palm City sometimes eat their lunch in the park _____ 12:00 P.M.

5. They also like to walk in the park _____ the evening.

6. The children always play in the playgrounds _____ June, July, and August.

7. You usually see them in the playgrounds _____ Friday and Saturday.

8. Palm City is also a nice place to visit _____ the winter.

9. Most of the time, the weather is warm _____ January.

10. The temperature is usually about 65 degrees _____ 8:00 A.M.

EXERCISE 3 Circle the correct preposition to complete each sentence.

Example: Stefan always visits Kenji at /(in) the summer.

1. He usually comes <u>in</u> / on August.

2. This year, he is coming <u>in</u> / on July 14.

3. His bus arrives <u>at</u> / in 10:00 A.M.

4. It arrives <u>in</u> / at night.

5. Kenji and Stefan are going to the museum <u>in</u> / on Sunday.

6. They're going <u>in</u> / at the afternoon.

7. They're going to the theater <u>in</u> / at the evening.

8. The show is <u>at</u> / on 8:30 P.M.

9. <u>In</u> / On two hours, they're going to the mall.

10. Stefan is going home <u>on</u> / at July 20.

11. Kenji wants to visit Stefan <u>in</u> / at May.

12. He likes to travel <u>on</u> / in the spring.

Name _____ Date _____

EXERCISE 4 Fill in each blank with the correct preposition.

Example: I usually go to bed late _____*at*_____ night.

I usually wake up (1) _____ 6:30 on school days. I take a shower, and

(2) _____ around 6:50 I eat breakfast. I always feel sleepy (3) _____

the morning. I catch my train (4) _____ 7:36. (5) _____ Mondays, the

train is very crowded. (6) _____ Fridays, I sometimes get a seat. I study English

(7) _____ the train. I have two classes (8)_____ the morning and one

(9) _____ the afternoon. I go to school (10) _____ 9:00

(11) _____ 3:30. I am at my job (12) _____ 4:30 (13) _____ 6:30.

I work at an ice cream shop, so I like my job (14) _____ the summer, but I hate my job

(15) _____ the winter. It's too cold!

EXERCISE 5 Underline the prepositions in each sentence. Circle the prepositional phrases.

Example: The audition was scheduled (for 9:30 A.M.)

1. Stephanie hadn't auditioned in months, so she was nervous.
2. The last audition she had was on a Saturday afternoon.
3. Last time, she had a chance to practice in the morning.
4. This time, her audition was in the morning, and she wanted to get there on time.
5. She also wanted to rehearse before her audition, so she got up at 7:00 A.M.
6. She rehearsed until 8:15 A.M. and left her house before 8:45 A.M.
7. She arrived in plenty of time.
8. She got the lead role and will be performing from Thursday to Sunday.
9. The play will begin at 8:00 P.M. in the evening.
10. She will have to arrive by 7:15 P.M. on the nights she performs.
11. Next month, another audition will be held.
12. She will make sure that she is on time then, too.

70

EXERCISE 6 Write *P* over the preposition in each sentence.

Example: It can be cold in the winter.
(P over "in")

1. In the winter, the days are short.

2. It gets dark early in the day.

3. There are some people who don't mind the cold in the wintertime.

4. There are some people who like it warm during the day.

5. Those people prefer the months that fall during the summer.

EXERCISE 7 Answer each question using prepositions of time. Use a long or short answer.

Example: When do you usually go to bed?
I usually go to bed at 11:30.   **or** *at 11:30*

1. When do you usually wake up? _____

2. What time do you eat breakfast? _____

3. What time do you leave for school? _____

4. What time does school start? _____

5. What time do you get home? _____

6. What time do you eat dinner? _____

7. When do you wake up on weekends? _____

8. When do you do your homework? _____

9. When do you talk on the telephone? _____

10. When do you use a computer? _____

11. When do you watch TV? _____

12. When is your birthday? _____

13. When is the most important holiday in your country? _____

14. When do you relax? _____

15. When is it cold in your country? _____

Grammar Focus

Use with student text page 264.

Recognize Commands with *Let*

EXAMPLE	USE
Get an application. **Let** them in. **Don't print** your name on the bottom line.	To give instructions
Please **show** me your driver's license. **Let** me see your homework. **Take** this card to the front desk, please.	To make a request
Don't open my mail. **Stand** at attention! **Don't be** late.	To make a command
Watch out! **Be** careful! **Don't** move!	To give a warning
Have a nice day. Please **let** yourself in. **Drive** safely.	In certain polite conversational expressions
Mind your own business!	In some angry, impolite expressions

LANGUAGE NOTES:

1. To form the imperative, use the base form. The subject of the imperative is *you*, but don't include *you* in the sentence.
2. A negative imperative is *do not* + base form. The contraction is *don't*.
3. An exclamation point (!) is used to show strong emotion.

EXERCISE 1 Explain the use of each imperative. Choose one for each.

Example: Wait for me! *B. To make a request*

A. To give instructions	B. To make a request	C. To make a command
D. To give a warning	E. In polite conversation	F. In impolite expression

1. Don't waste time. _____

2. Take care of yourself. _____

3. Be quiet! _____

4. Open the door. _____

5. Steady now! _____

6. Relax and stay a while. _____

7. Be good! _____

8. Take out your books. _____

9. Please tell me the way to the post office. _____

10. Stop where you are! _____

11. Please don't worry about it. _____

12. Get away from me! _____

13. Turn to page 9 in the book. _____

14. Take your time. _____

15. Let me see! _____

EXERCISE 2 Fill in each blank with an appropriate imperative verb (affirmative or negative) to give instructions on how to be a good language learner.

Example: _Practice_____ your pronunciation.

1. _____ questions.
2. _____ with native speakers.
3. _____ your homework.
4. _____ be absent.
5. _____ your textbook.
6. _____ your notebook.
7. _____ notes.
8. _____ to your teacher.
9. _____ in class.
10. _____ your best.

EXERCISE 3 Fill in each blank with an appropriate imperative verb (affirmative or negative) to give instructions on how to behave in a job interview.

Example: _Don't wear_____ strange clothes.

1. _____ late.
2. _____ nice clothes.
3. _____ your resume.
4. _____ a pen to fill out the application.
5. _____ gum.
6. _____ the interviewer's questions.
7. _____ to smile.
8. _____ politely.

EXERCISE 4 Look at the sentences in Exercise 3. Rewrite each affirmative sentence in the negative and each negative sentence in the affirmative.

Example: *Wear strange clothes.*

1. _____
2. _____
3. _____
4. _____
5. _____
6. _____
7. _____
8. _____

EXERCISE 5 Choose a verb from the box to complete each sentence. Use the negative form when indicated. More than one answer is often possible.

read	listen	ask	don't put
help	write	don't use	don't eat
don't take	don't cook	cut	

Example: ___Help___ your sister make dinner.

1. _____ the server about the menu.
2. _____ the shopping list.
3. _____ my bowl.
4. _____ to your parents.
5. _____ eggs in the microwave.
6. _____ candy all day.
7. _____ the carrots in half.
8. _____ a check for the food.
9. _____ the dog to the restaurant.
10. _____ pennies in the vending machine.

EXERCISE 6 Underline the imperatives in each sentence.

Example: Listen to the birds chirp.

1. Sit on the bench.
2. Enjoy the weather.
3. Let him see what you brought for lunch.
4. Buy me a bottle of water.
5. Take the money for the food.

EXERCISE 7 Underline the imperatives in the following paragraph. The first one is done for you.

Here are the directions to get to my new apartment from the bank. <u>Go</u> north on Emerson Street. Walk straight ahead for two blocks. There is a pharmacy on the left. Turn left on Michigan Avenue. Go two blocks. At the intersection of Michigan Avenue and Lincoln Street, turn right. Don't turn left; that's the way to my old apartment. My new apartment is at the end of Lincoln Street, on the left. Walk up the stairs. Find apartment #3.

EXERCISE 8 Silvia's mom is getting ready for a party. Read the instructions she gives Silvia and her brother. Fill in each imperative. Use the negative form when indicated.

Example: _Don't watch_ TV now.
(watch, negative)

I need your help. Please _____ the rug and _____ your rooms. _____
(1. vacuum) (2. clean) (3. eat, negative)

the snacks in the living room. _____ eggs, milk and bread. _____ the food at the
(4. buy) (5. buy, negative)

convenience store. _____ to Food City. _____ and _____ the potatoes.
(6. go) (7. Peel) (8. whip)

_____ a salad. _____ and _____ the lettuce first. Then
(9. make) (10. wash) (11.drain)

_____ the table. _____ the blue plates. Use the white plates. _____
(12. set) (13. use, negative) (14. choose)

some pretty napkins. _____ on some nice clothes.
(15. put)

EXERCISE 9 If the sentence is affirmative, make it negative. If it is negative, make it affirmative.

Examples: Complete the application now. _Don't complete the application now._
Don't turn right on Oak Street. _Turn right on Oak Street._

1. Go to the post office today. _____
2. Write your address on the form. _____
3. Don't send the package economy class. _____
4. Don't buy insurance for the package. _____
5. Fill in all the customs forms now. _____

Name _____ Date _____

Grammar Focus

Use with student text page 278.

Recognize Reported Speech

EXAMPLE	EXPLANATION
Before the 1940s experts told parents **that they should be strict with their kids.** They said **that too much affection wasn't good for the child.**	Reported speech is used to paraphrase or summarize what someone has said. We don't remember the exact words because they weren't recorded. The ideas are more important than the exact words.
Sentence with exact quote: 　She said, "I will help you tomorrow." • Quotation marks • Comma after said • Doesn't contain *that* • Pronoun = *I* • Verb = *will help* • Time = *tomorrow*	Sentence with reported speech: 　She said that she would help me the next day. • No quotation marks • No comma after said • Contains *that* (optional) • Pronouns = *she, me* • Verb = *would help* • Time = *the next day*

LANGUAGE NOTES:

1. Other time changes from exact quote to reported speech:
   today = that day　now = then　yesterday = the day before
   last night = the night before

2. In most cases, reported speech shifts verb tenses to the past of the current form:
   She asked, "Can you help me move this morning?"
   She asked if I could help her move that morning.

3. A reported question ends in a period, not a question mark.
   He asked, "Is she a teacher?"
   He asked if she was a teacher.

EXERCISE 1 Underline the reported speech in each of the following sentences.

Example: I told my friend that I wanted to leave the party.

1. She said that she was thinking about doing the same thing.

2. One friend told us she was going to be driving home and we could have a ride.

3. We told her that we'd be grateful for a ride.

4. The hostess at the party said she was glad we had come.

5. We said that it was one of the best parties we had been to in a long time.

6. We told her we wanted to leave because we were tired.

7. My friend said she hoped she'd have another party soon.

8. We told her it was a great idea.

9. On the way home my friend said that she'd go back to a party there any time.

10. I said that I could have a party at my house one day.

76

Name _____ Date _____

EXERCISE 2 Change each of the exact quotes to reported speech. Follow the examples.

Examples: My friend called me and asked, "Are you busy over the weekend?"

My friend called and asked if I was busy over the weekend.

I said, "I'm not busy at all."

I said that I wasn't busy at all.

1. I asked, "Why are you asking?"

2. She said, "I have an extra ticket for a show tomorrow."

3. She said, "I'd love to have you join me."

4. I said, "My only plans for tomorrow will be to study."

5. She said, "That sounds a little boring. You should join me."

6. I said, "I'd love to go if I can pay for the ticket."

EXERCISE 3 Change each reported speech to an exact quote.

Example: My friend in Japan called and said that she had some happy news to tell me.

My friend in Japan called and said, "I have some happy news to tell you."

1. She said that she had just gotten a new job teaching English at a university.

2. I asked her how she got the job.

3. She said she had seen the posting for the job in a language journal.

4. I told her she was lucky to get such a good job.

5. She said that she agreed and that she was very lucky.

6. She asked me how I was doing.

77

Name _____ Date _____

EXERCISE 4 Change each *yes / no* question to reported speech.

Example: The student asked, "Is that woman our new teacher?"

The student asked if that woman was our new teacher.

1. My friend asked, "Do we have to do the homework tonight?"

   _____

2. Her parents asked her, "Are you going out alone?"

   _____

3. The child asked, "Have you seen my mother?"

   _____

4. Her friend asked her, "Did you remember to bring your CDs?"

   _____

5. The man in the store asked, "Is there something I can help you find?"

   _____

EXERCISE 5 Change the words in parentheses to reported speech.

(**Example 1**) The little boy was playing in his yard when he shouted (There's a wolf here.)

that there was a wolf there . (**Example 2**) His father ran out and asked (Where is the wolf?)

where the wolf was . (1) The boy laughed and said (I'm only joking.)

_____ . (2) His father got angry and said (Don't do that again.)

_____ . But the boy did it again. (3) This time he said (There

really is a wolf here. Please believe me.) _____ . His father came

running out only to find that there was no wolf anywhere. (4) He returned to the house and as he

left he asked the boy (How can I ever believe you?) _____ .

(5) A little while later a wolf did approach the boy, and the boy shouted (I see a wolf!)

_____ . (6) His father asked (Do you expect me to believe you?)

_____ , and he went back to his work. (7) After a while when

he didn't hear the boy, he asked (What are you doing?) _____ .

(8) When the boy did not answer, he ran out and cried (Where are you?)

_____ . But it was too late. The boy had been eaten by the wolf.

VISIONS A Grammar Practice • Copyright © Thomson Heinle

Name _____ Date _____

EXERCISE 6 Change each reported speech sentence to an exact quote.

Example: The teacher warned them not to be late.

The teacher warned, "Don't be late."

1. His parents asked him not to turn up his music.

   _____

2. Her parents asked her to come home early from the party.

   _____

3. The principal informed the students that school would finish at noon the next day.

   _____

4. The teacher reminded the students to bring their dictionaries to class.

   _____

5. His friends convinced him to go to the movies with them.

   _____

6. Her father taught her to respect other people.

   _____

7. The teacher assured the students that there would be no homework.

   _____

8. His friend advised him not to worry so much.

   _____

EXERCISE 7 Complete each of the following expressions with reported speech.

Example: My parents told me *not to talk to strangers.*

1. My best friend asked me _____

2. Our teacher told us _____

3. The speaker asked the audience _____

4. Her mom asked her _____

5. Someone I know told me _____

6. They asked us _____

7. I asked you _____

8. You told me _____

Grammar Focus

Use with student text page 296.

Recognize and Use the Simple Past Tense

BASE	PAST	EXAMPLE
walk	walked	I **walked** two miles every day last week.
talk	talked	You **talked** to the doctor yesterday.
play	played	He/She **played** soccer once a week.
exercise	exercised	We **exercised** on Saturday.
reduce	reduced	They **reduced** their blood pressure.

LANGUAGE NOTES:

1. The past tense form of regular verbs is the same for all persons.
2. For most verbs ending in a consonant, add **-ed: worked.**
3. If the base ends in a vowel, add **-d: lived.**
4. If the base ends in a vowel + **y**, do *not* change the **y: stayed.**
5. For a one-syllable verb ending in *consonant + vowel + consonant*, double the final consonant and add **-ed: stopped.**

BASE	SUBJECT	PAST	EXAMPLE
be	I he, she, it	was	I **was** a patient. He, She, It **was** tired.
	we you they	were	We **were** nervous. You **were** in the hospital. They **were** at the doctor's office.
have	I you he, she, it we they	had	I **had** a fever. You **had** a stomachache. He, She, It **had** a broken leg. We **had** high blood pressure. They **had** an appointment at 3:00.

LANGUAGE NOTE:

The past tense of verbs like *be* and *have* take the irregular form.

EXERCISE 1 Write the simple past tense of each verb.

Example: smoke _____*smoked*_____

1. chew _____
2. continue _____
3. shop _____
4. look _____
5. like _____
6. miss _____

7. move _____   10. exercise _____

8. need _____   11. want _____

9. stay _____   12. live _____

EXERCISE 2 Complete each sentence with the simple past tense of the verb in parentheses.

Example: (exercise) Last week, Alex _____*exercised*_____ every day.

1. (play) He also _____ tennis on Saturday.

2. (want) His wife, Irina, _____ to play tennis on Saturday, too.

3. (visit) On Sunday, she _____ her mother, Anya.

4. (ask) The children _____ to go to the miniature golf course on Saturday afternoon.

5. (stay) They _____ until 5:00.

6. (walk) Last Saturday, I _____ five miles with my sister.

7. (need) We _____ to get some exercise.

8. (lower) My sister _____ her blood pressure by walking every day.

9. (exercise) You _____ a lot last year.

10. (stop) But you _____ last month.

EXERCISE 3 Circle the correct simple past verb form for each sentence.

Example: Last year, Luc has /(had) some health problems.

1. He <u>was / were</u> in the hospital a lot.

2. His wife <u>be / was</u> very nervous.

3. I <u>were / was</u> very healthy last year.

4. I <u>had / having</u> a good exercise plan.

5. You <u>were / was</u> sick last week.

6. You <u>had / having</u> a headache.

7. My brother and I <u>has / had</u> a bad day yesterday.

8. We <u>was / were</u> both very tired.

9. My dog <u>had / have</u> a broken leg last year.

10. The children <u>was / were</u> very sad about it.

EXERCISE 4 Use the each group of words to write a simple past tense sentence.

Example: Yesterday I / be / tired during the day   *Yesterday I was tired during the day.*

1. I / have / a stomachache, too   _____

2. you / be / sick last week   _____

3. you / have / a cough and a fever   _____

4. this morning Ken / be / nervous   _____

5. he / have / a bad headache   _____

6. Mr. and Mrs. Ito / have / a lot of health problems _____

7. we / be / very healthy _____

8. we / have / checkups in May _____

EXERCISE 5 Fill in each blank with *was* or *were*.

Example: My mother ___was___ a homemaker.

1. I _____ self-employed in my country. 4. _____ the bus boy busy?

2. _____ he in the office yesterday? 5. _____ you good students last semester?

3. The copy machine _____ broken. 6. _____ the workers in the cafeteria?

EXERCISE 6 Complete each sentence with the simple past tense of the verb in parentheses.

Example: He (have) work experience. *He had work experience.* _____

1. My father (work) the night shift. _____

2. He (explain) the benefits. _____

3. The bus boy (clean) the tables. _____

4. I (cook) hamburgers in a restaurant. _____

5. Ricardo (complete) a job application. _____

6. The company (hire) a new employee. _____

EXERCISE 7 Rewrite the sentences below, changing each verb to a simple past tense verb.

Example: I need a ticket. *I needed a ticket.* _____

1. I live in a small house. _____

2. We need money. _____

3. He starts school on Monday. _____

4. They offer me a ride. _____

5. Chris fixes my computer. _____

6. The tree moves in the wind. _____

7. The automatic doors open. _____

8. Joanna looks out the window. _____

9. The cat cries at the door. _____

10. We open the presents. _____

EXERCISE 8 Use each group of words to write a sentence in the simple past tense.

Example: you / paint / safety signs *You painted the safety signs.*

1. Ricardo / manage / 22 employees

    _____

2. the salespeople / improve / their product knowledge

    _____

3. her friend / apply / for the job

    _____

4. the taxi driver / park / carefully

    _____

5. they / dress / well / for the party

    _____

EXERCISE 9 Kazuhiro is asking his friend, Isabella, about her last job. Answer Kazuhiro's questions using sentences with the past tense of *be*.

Example: Kazuhiro: (be / you / happy / at your job) *Were you happy at your job?*
          Isabella: (yes / I / be) *Yes, I was.*

1. Kazuhiro: Was it a full-time job?
2. Isabella: (yes / it / be) _____
3. Kazuhiro: Were your co-workers friendly?
4. Isabella: Yes. (my manager / be / nice / too) _____
5. Kazuhiro: Were the benefits good?
6. Isabella: (yes / they / be / great) _____We had three weeks vacation.
7. Kazuhiro: Was the work boring?
8. Isabella: (no, it / be [negative]) _____
9. Kazuhiro: Was the office far away?
10. Isabella: (no / it / be [negative]) _____ I walked to work.
11. Kazuhiro: I want to work there! Was the salary okay?
12. Isabella: (the salary / be / high) _____
              But, sorry, the job was in Brazil!

Grammar Focus

Use with student text page 310.

Use Dependent Clauses with *Because*

EXAMPLE	TYPE OF CLAUSE
I went to Guatemala **before I went to Belize.**	Time clause
I went to Guatemala **because I wanted to visit my friend.**	Reason clause
I also went there **so that I could study Spanish.**	Purpose clause
I came here **even though I didn't know Spanish.**	Contrast clause
I will go back to my country for vacation **if I save enough money.**	Condition clause

LANGUAGE NOTES:

1. An adverbial clause is dependent on the main clause for its meaning. It must be attached to the main clause:

   Wrong: She didn't come to class. Because she was sick.
   Right: She didn't come to class because she was sick.

2. A dependent clause can come before or after the main clause. If the dependent clause comes before the main clause, it is usually separated from the main clause with a comma. Compare the following:

   I went to Guatemala before I went to Belize. (no comma)
   Before I went to Belize, I went to Guatemala. (comma)

EXERCISE 1 Read the following sentences with adverbial clauses. Underline and identify the type of clause found in each sentence: *time, reason, purpose, contrast,* or *condition.*

Example: He went to France <u>even though he didn't know anybody there.</u> _____*contrast*_____

1. He got a lot of information about France before he left. _____

2. He went alone so that he could meet as many people as possible. _____

3. He wanted to go because he has always enjoyed studying French. _____

4. His parents had told him he could go if he saved enough money for the trip. _____

5. If he found a job there, he could stay even longer. _____

6. Even though he didn't have much money, he was sure he could find a way to stay there. _____

7. He began looking for possible jobs on the Internet before he left. _____

8. Because he could speak French well, he was sure he could get a job. _____

EXERCISE 2 Insert the appropriate adverbial clause word where needed. Choose an expression for each blank: *before / because / even though / so that*.

She decided to travel to China (**Example**) _____*because*_____ she had always been

interested in Chinese culture. (1) _____ her family was Canadian, she had always

wanted to go. She started studying Chinese at school (2) _____ she could speak

Chinese. (3) _____ she got good grades, her parents told her they would help

her with the trip. Her best friend also studied Chinese (4) _____ she could go too.

(5) _____ they left on their trip, they were very excited.

EXERCISE 3 Match each main clause with a dependent clause to make a sentence. Make the type of dependent clause stated in parentheses.

Main Clauses	Dependent Clauses
She went to Italy	because she has enough money.
She studied Italian	~~before she studied English.~~
She will go back to Italy	even though she was only 15.
	so that she can visit Rome and Florence.
	because her family is Italian.
	because she wanted to.
	even though she gets homesick.
	after she learned Italian.
	so that she could get an international job.

Example: (time) *She studied Italian before she studied English.* _____

1. (reason) _____
2. (purpose) _____
3. (contrast) _____
4. (condition) _____
5. (time) _____
6. (reason) _____
7. (purpose) _____
8. (time) _____

Name _____ Date _____

EXERCISE 4 Fill in each blank using *because* or *so that*. Then circle the dependent clause.

Example: Felicia's mom wants to get a job ⟨ _____so that_____ she can help her family.⟩

Felicia's mom can't get a job now (1) _____ she has children at home. She can get a job next year (2) _____ the children will be in school. She is studying computers (3) _____ she can get a good job.

Lam's grandfather can't send his grandchildren to college (4) _____ it is too expensive. He is thinking about borrowing money (5) _____ they can attend. His grandchildren may get jobs (6) _____ they can help pay for college.

EXERCISE 5 Use an item from each column to write sentences with *because* and *so that* about Luisa.

~~Luisa leaves the house at 8:30~~	she would not get cold
she takes the bus	she would get to work early
she wore a coat	it's cheaper than a taxi
she didn't take an umbrella	~~she gets to work at 9:00~~
her daughter stayed home	it wasn't raining
today she left home at 8:00	she was sick

Example: _Luisa leaves the house at 8:30 so that she gets to work at 9:00._

1. _____
2. _____
3. _____
4. _____
5. _____

EXERCISE 6 Fill in each blank using *because, before, even though,* or *so that*.

Example: Mark and Jasmine hadn't seen each other all summer _even though_ they are best friends.

Mark and Jasmine will be able to get together more often (1) _____ school will be starting soon. Mark and Jasmine meet at the library (2) _____ they walk to school together. Mark and Jasmine meet every morning (3) _____ it is very early. Mark joined the student government (4) _____ he and Jasmine could participate in the same organization.

VISIONS A Grammar Practice • Copyright © Thomson Heinle

EXERCISE 7   Complete each sentence using *because, before, even though,* or *so that.*

Example: Ms. Nathaniel teaches an ESL course *because* she likes helping people learn English.

1. Shanti decided to take ESL II _____ she could improve her English skills.

2. Students had to take ESL I _____ they could take ESL II.

3. Shanti enrolled in Ms. Nathaniel's ESL II class _____ she heard that Ms. Nathaniel was a good teacher.

4. Shanti practiced the things she learned in ESL I _____ Ms. Nathaniel's class started.

5. Shanti did her ESL II homework every night _____ she could get a good grade.

6. Shanti worked with a tutor _____ she did well on her assignments.

7. Ms. Nathaniel stayed after class _____ some students needed extra help.

8. Shanti got an 'A' in her ESL II class _____ Ms. Nathaniel's class was often challenging and difficult.

EXERCISE 8   Rewrite each sentence in Exercise 7 so that the dependent clause is at the beginning of each sentence. Make sure to put a comma after the dependent clause.

Example: *Because she likes helping people learn English, Ms. Nathaniel teaches an ESL course.*

1. _____
   _____

2. _____
   _____

3. _____
   _____

4. _____
   _____

5. _____
   _____

6. _____
   _____

7. _____
   _____

8. _____
   _____

VISIONS A Grammar Practice • Copyright © Thomson Heinle

VISIONS Unit 5 • Chapter 2 The Fun They Had

Grammar Focus

Use with student text page 324.

Use *Might* to Show Possibility

VISIONS Unit 5 • Chapter 3 Using the Scientific Method

EXAMPLE	EXPLANATION
I **may** go out for dinner tonight. I **might** have Chinese food. I **may** go to Europe in the fall. If you don't study, you **might** fail.	*May* and *might* have the same meaning. They show possibility.

EXERCISE 1 Fill in each blank with a verb to express what *may* or *might* happen or be true.

Example: It is cloudy today. It might _____*rain*_____ this afternoon.

1. The baby is playing with a coin. She might _____ it.
2. The dog is barking a lot. It might _____ hungry.
3. I don't know what we are going to do tonight. We may _____ home.
4. Mom's upstairs working. She might _____ the phone.
5. Kenny's forehead feels hot. He may _____ a fever.
6. George is a half hour late. He might _____ lost.
7. Carol went out. She may _____ at the store.
8. This is a no-parking zone. We may _____ a ticket.
9. I need a present for Charles. I might _____ him a CD player.
10. I may _____ my friend at the movie theater later.

EXERCISE 2 Write what *may* or *might* happen in each of the following situations.

Example: If you get a new job, *you might make more money.* _____

1. If you come to class every day, _____
2. If you make too much noise in your apartment, _____
3. If you smile at someone on the street, _____

VISIONS A Grammar Practice • Copyright © Thomson Heinle

Name _____ Date _____

4. If you go to a foreign country, _____

5. If you never practice English, _____

6. If you eat very healthy foods, _____

7. If you meet and fall in love, _____

8. If you move to a different city, _____

9. If you go shopping this weekend, _____

10. If you eat too many sweets, _____

EXERCISE 3 Fill in each blank with *may, might, may not* or *might not* to make true statements about your future.

Example: I _____*might not*_____ get married.

1. I _____ have many (more) classmates.

2. I _____ get a (new) job.

3. I _____ live in another country.

4. I _____ go to college.

5. I _____ be very successful.

6. I _____ write a book.

7. I _____ make a movie.

8. I _____ travel around the world.

9. I _____ learn another language.

10. I _____ become famous.

EXERCISE 4 Complete each sentence.

1. Next year I may _____

2. In a month I might _____

3. Tomorrow I might _____

4. Tonight I may not _____

5. Today I might not _____

6. This year might not _____

EXERCISE 5 Write sentences to introduce each of the following situations.

Example: _My friends couldn't come to dinner Friday at 5:30 P.M._

My friends might come to dinner Friday at 6:30 P.M.

1. _____

You might get a wonderful job when you graduate from college.

2. _____

The world may become peaceful for the next one hundred years.

3. _____

All the students may get excellent grades on the final exam.

4. _____

She may have a hair salon appointment at 5:00 P.M.

5. _____

We may have a little rain tonight. The forecast wasn't clear.

6. _____

I don't really know. They might move to Venezuela next year.

7. _____

I may come to see you tomorrow morning at 9:30 A.M.

8. _____

Your car sounds a little strange. You might have to go to the mechanic.

9. _____

My first paycheck might arrive tomorrow.

10. _____

George and Debbie may marry on June 21.

EXERCISE 6 Write what may or might happen in each of the following situations.

Example: My cat isn't in the house. _He may be hiding._

1. Their television isn't on. Her husband _____

2. The newspaper said we _____

3. Your forehead feels hot. You _____

4. Many people were sick at school. You _____

5. I'm not good at math. I _____

6. She loves to travel. She _____

EXERCISE 7 Write ten sentences about what you *may / might* do in the coming year.

Example: *I may learn to ride a bicycle.*

1. _____
2. _____
3. _____
4. _____
5. _____
6. _____
7. _____
8. _____
9. _____
10. _____

EXERCISE 8 Write ten sentences about things that you *may not / might not* do in the future.

Example: *I may not find an inexpensive apartment.*

1. _____
2. _____
3. _____
4. _____
5. _____
6. _____
7. _____
8. _____
9. _____
10. _____

Grammar Focus

Use with student text page 342.

Identify Superlative Adjectives

	SIMPLE	SUPERLATIVE
One-syllable adjectives and adverbs	tall	the tallest
	fast	the fastest
	sad	the saddest
	big	the biggest
Two-syllable adjectives that end in −y	easy	the easiest
	happy	the happiest
(Note spelling changes in words ending in −y.)		
Other two-syllable adjectives	frequent	the most frequent
	active	the most active
Some two-syllable adjectives have two forms	simple	the simplest
		the most simple
(Other two-syllable adjectives that have two forms are *handsome, quiet, gentle, narrow, clever, common, friendly, angry, polite, stupid*.)		
Adjectives with three or more syllables	important	the most important
	difficult	the most difficult
−*ly* adverbs	quickly	the most quickly
Irregular adjectives / adverbs	good / well	the best
	bad / badly	the worst
	far	the farthest
	little	the least
	a lot	the most

LANGUAGE NOTE:

Bored and *tired* are considered two-syllable adjectives and use *more* and *the most* in the comparative form.

I am *more tired* than you today.
I am *the most tired* of our whole team.

EXERCISE 1 For each simple adjective, write the superlative adjective.

Example: cold   _coldest_____

1. good   _____
2. fast   _____
3. polite   _____
4. bad   _____
5. busy   _____
6. quiet   _____
7. intelligent   _____
8. lazy   _____
9. friendly   _____
10. famous   _____
11. ugly   _____
12. old   _____

EXERCISE 2 Answer each of the following questions with a complete sentence.

Example: **Q:** What is the most beautiful city in your country?

A: _I think Madrid is the most beautiful city in my country._____

1. **Q:** Who is one of the most popular singers in your country?

   A: _____

2. **Q:** What is your hardest subject in school?

   A: _____

3. **Q:** Who is one of the happiest people that you know?

   A: _____

4. **Q:** What was one of the most important inventions of the twentieth century?

   A: _____

5. **Q:** What time does your first class start?

   A: _____

6. **Q:** Who is one of the most famous people in the world?

   A: _____

7. **Q:** What is the saddest movie that you've ever seen?

   A: _____

EXERCISE 3 Complete each statement with a superlative adjective from the box.

easiest	wisest	rarest	largest	fastest	tallest
worst	silliest	shortest	greatest	smallest	

Example: The Sears Tower is one of the world's _____*tallest*_____ buildings.

1. Gandhi was one of the _____ people who ever lived.
2. The tiger is one of the _____ animals in the world.
3. February is the _____ month of the year.
4. Jupiter is the _____ of all the planets.
5. Monaco is one of the _____ countries in the world.
6. Comedies can be the _____ kind of movies.
7. Picasso was one of the _____ painters of his time.
8. The cheetah is the _____ animal on four legs.
9. The mosquito is one of the _____ insects.
10. E-mail is one of the _____ forms of communication.

EXERCISE 4 Rewrite each sentence using the correct form of the superlative adjective.

Example: Ramon always did the (nice) things for his family.
Ramon always did the nicest things for his family.

1. This time, Ramon planned to cook his family the (good) dinner they have ever had.

_____

2. The local supermarket has the (large) selection of produce in the town.

_____

3. Ramon bought the (fresh) produce he could find.

_____

4. He prepared the (elegant) meal he has ever prepared.

_____

5. His family was the (full) they had ever been.

_____

Name _____ Date _____

EXERCISE 5 Rewrite each sentence using the superlative form of the adjective in parentheses.

Example: Ms. Davison assigned the (hard) assignment so far this year.

Ms. Davison assigned the *hardest* assignment so far this year.

1. The class had to write about the (important) thing they ever did.

   _____

2. Students were the (challenge) they had been all year.

   _____

3. Harrison was the (excited) he had been about any assignment.

   _____

4. "This is going to be the (easy) assignment ever," Harrison thought to himself.

   _____

5. Harrison wrote the (long) essay of anyone in the class.

   _____

6. His essay talked about the (great) gift he ever gave another person.

   _____

7. Harrison worked the (long) hours he had ever worked.

   _____

8. He helped build the (beautiful) house he had ever seen.

   _____

9. The house was given to the (nice) family he has ever met.

   _____

10. That day, he was the (happy) person on earth.

   _____

11. Ms. Davison was the (impressed) she had ever been with a student's work.

   _____

12. Ms. Davison told Harrison that building a house was the (generous) thing any of her students had ever done.

   _____

13. Harrison said that it was the (hard), (gratify) thing he was ever involved with.

   _____

Grammar Focus

Use with student text page 360.

Identify Possessive Adjectives

SUBJECT PRONOUN	POSSESSIVE ADJECTIVE	EXAMPLE
I	my	I like **my** name.
you	your	You're a new student. What's **your** name?
he	his	He likes **his** name.
she	her	She doesn't like **her** name.
it	its	Is this your dog? Is it friendly? What's **its** name?
we	our	We use **our** nicknames.
they	their	They are new friends. **Their** last name is Jackson.

LANGUAGE NOTES:

1. Possessive adjectives come before a noun and show possession.
2. Be careful not to confuse *his* and *her*:

   My mother lives in Chicago. *Her* brother lives in Las Vegas.

EXERCISE 1 Fill in each blank with the correct subject, pronoun, or possessive adjective from the choices enclosed in parentheses.

Example: (his / he) In the morning, _____*he*_____ washes _____*his*_____ face.

1. (my / I) _____ mother and _____ went shopping this week.
2. (they / their) _____ family visits when _____ have a vacation.
3. (our / we) _____ love _____ new apartment.
4. (her / she) _____ bought a tree for _____ garden.
5. (it / its) _____ looks great in _____ new place by the roses.
6. (your / you) _____ and _____ brother look just the same!
7. (he / his) _____ buys _____ jackets at an expensive store.
8. (I / my) _____ teacher and _____ solve many math problems.
9. (their / they) _____ grades aren't so good. _____ usually do better.
10. (we / our) _____ want to read _____ books tonight.
11. (its / it) _____ paw is hurt and _____ needs medical attention.
12. (she / her) _____ rides the bus to _____ job on weekdays.
13. (you / your) _____ dinner is ready. Are _____ ready to eat?

14. (his / he) _____ watches _____ favorite show on Fridays.

15. (my / I) _____ always lose _____ watch.

16. (they / their) _____ and _____ parents cook wonderful meals.

EXERCISE 2 Fill in each blank with the possessive adjectives that refer to the subject.

Example: I like _____*my*_____ teacher.

1. He opens _____ book.

2. She loves _____ grandfather.

3. The cat likes _____ toy.

4. Many teachers give _____ students too much homework.

5. Sometimes my sister does _____ homework in the bathtub.

6. Mr. Johnson buys _____ shoes in the spring.

7. Do you use _____ dictionary every day?

8. I bring _____ daughter to work with me sometimes.

9. We wear _____ coats in winter.

10. Ms. Winfrey always tells _____ children to eat _____ dinner.

11. Some people wash _____ cars every day.

12. He uses _____ cell phone in class.

13. She keeps _____ pencils in _____ bag.

14. The mouse eats _____ cheese.

15. Most people love _____ parents.

16. Sometimes Lisa eats _____ lunch in the morning.

17. I carry _____ bag everywhere.

18. We need _____ books now.

19. She eats _____ lunch at the same time every day.

20. Two of my friends do _____ homework together.

21. He talks to _____ grandmother every week on the phone.

22. The computer needs _____ hard drive.

23. You often clean _____ car.

24. You always buy _____ shoes at the department store.

25. We usually call _____ grandparents on Sunday.

26. Does he want _____ test grade now?

27. This bag always breaks at _____ strap.

28. I am hungry for _____ lunch right now.

EXERCISE 3 Complete each sentence with the possessive adjective that refers to the subject.

Example: Steve likes __*his*__ new hat.

1. She wears _____ jeans to work.
2. You buy all _____ clothes at Porter's.
3. I shop for _____ clothes at The Boutique.
4. The cat wears _____ sweater all the time.
5. We need _____ coats in the winter.

6. Mario and _____ family often wear shorts.
7. They use _____ coupons to buy clothes.
8. The children wear _____ T-shirts to school.
9. You never wear _____ hat in the summer.
10. I don't have _____ receipt from the store.

EXERCISE 4 Choose the correct word to complete each sentence. Mark the correct bubble. Fill in the bubble completely.

			A	B
Example: I like _____ striped shirt.	A. we	B. my	○	●
1. Lien wants _____ plaid jacket.	A. she	B. her	○	○
2. Where do they buy _____ shoes?	A. their	B. he	○	○
3. You always wear a green shirt with _____ brown pants.	A. your	B. its	○	○
4. Vladimir and Ziven wear _____ blue backpacks to school.	A. they	B. their	○	○
5. We don't wear _____ expensive shoes to the beach.	A. our	B. you	○	○
6. When it snows, the dog wears _____ flowered sweater.	A. its	B. it	○	○
7. It's rainy today. I need _____ raincoat.	A. its	B. my	○	○
8. The dress is $20.00 off _____ regular price.	A. its	B. her	○	○
9. We always buy _____ winter clothes at the mall.	A. we	B. our	○	○
10. Kenji never wears _____ red tie.	A. he	B. his	○	○
11. Do you want _____ shorts and T-shirt?	A. your	B. you	○	○
12. Does Marie wear _____ scarf in the winter?	A. she	B. her	○	○

EXERCISE 5 Roberto is talking about his family. Complete each sentence with a possessive adjective.

Example: I have a sister. _____*Her*_____ name is Silvia.

1. I have two siblings. _____ siblings are in high school.
2. My brother is 17. _____ name is Juan.
3. My sister is 15. _____ name is Carla.
4. Juan and Carla both have nice eyes. _____ eyes are brown.
5. My mother has nice eyes, too. _____ eyes are green.
6. My mother and Carla both have long hair. _____ hair is black.
7. You have five sisters and two brothers? _____ family is large!
8. My sister and I are students at Elm Street High School. _____ school has many new students.

Name _____ Date _____

EXERCISE 6 Complete each sentence in the paragraph with a possessive adjective.

Example: _____*My*_____ name is Helena.

This is a photo of _____ family. This is my sister. _____ name is Ana.
                        (1)   (2)

Ana has two children, Rosalina and Luiz. They are twins, a girl and a boy. _____ birthday is
                                                                                    (3)

August 8. Rosalina has blue eyes and _____ hair is red. Luiz has brown eyes and
                                              (4)

_____ hair is brown. Rosalina likes movies and books. _____ favorite books are
      (5)   (6)

about family life. Luiz loves _____ dog. He takes _____ dog to the park every
                                    (7)   (8)

day. My brother and I love _____ family. We think _____ neice and nephew are
                                  (9)   (10)

very smart and good-looking. Of course, they think _____ aunt and uncle are smart and
                                                            (11)

good-looking, too! Do you have a picture of _____ family?
                                                    (12)

EXERCISE 7 Fill in each blank with a possessive adjective that refers to the subject.

Example: Jilani loves _____*his*_____ dog.

1. Jilani walks _____ dog every morning.
2. Daisy always wears _____ leash.
3. They both look forward to _____ walks.
4. Jilani ran into _____ friend, Dana.
5. "What's _____ name?" asked Dana.
6. "Daisy is _____ name," Jilani replied.
7. Thank goodness Daisy is acting _____ best, Jilani thought to himself.
8. "Well, I should get to _____ appointment," said Dana.
9. "We should go back to _____ house, too," said Jilani.
10. "I'll see you tomorrow in _____ math class," said Dana.

VISIONS A Grammar Practice • Copyright © Thomson Heinle

VISIONS Unit 6 • Chapter 1 Esperanza Rising

99

Grammar Focus

Use with student text page 376.

Understand the Past Perfect Tense

EXAMPLE	USES OF THE PAST PERFECT
We **had seen** the movie before.	Past perfect = *had* + past participle.
By the time the rescue ship arrived, the *Titanic* **had** already **gone** down.	To show that something happened before a specific date, time, or event.
When people got on the lifeboats, the rescue ship **hadn't arrived** yet.	To show that something happened or didn't happen before the verb in the *when* clause.
There was a lot of ice in the water because the previous winter **had been** unusually mild in the Arctic.	After *because*, to show a prior reason.
The captain didn't realize how close his ship **had come** to the iceberg.	In a noun clause, when the main verb is past.
The passengers in third class were emigrants who **had left** behind their old way of life.	In a *who / that / which* clause, to show a prior action.
Many emigrants on the *Titanic* **had** never **left** their homelands before.	With *never . . . before*, in relation to a past time.
The ship **had been** at sea for five days when it hit an iceberg.	With *for*, to show the duration of an earlier past action.

LANGUAGE NOTES:

1. To form the past perfect tense, use *had/had not (hadn't)* + past participle.
   I *had sent* my resume last month.
   I *had not (hadn't) received* a response before today.
2. The past participle of regular verbs is formed by adding *-d* or *-ed* to the base form of the verb.
   close - clos*ed*   stay - stay*ed*
3. The past participles of some irregular verbs include: be - been, buy - bought, find - found, forget - forgotten, hear - heard, leave - left, lose - lost, meet - met, say - said, see - seen, take - taken, teach - taught, think - thought.

EXERCISE 1 Fill in each blank with the past perfect tense of the verb.

Example: look   *had looked*

1. teach   _____
2. buy   _____

Name _____ Date _____

3. meet _____
4. finish _____
5. shop _____
6. work _____
7. listen _____

EXERCISE 2 Complete each sentence with the past perfect tense of the verb in parentheses.

Example: I couldn't buy something to eat because I (forget) _____*had forgotten*_____ my wallet.

1. She didn't know the words to the song because she (never / hear) _____ it.

2. When they arrived at the theater, the movie (already / start) _____.

3. They (be) _____ on vacation for one week when they arrived in Paris.

4. By the time he called the fire department, his house (burn) _____ to the ground.

5. The team was made up of friends who (play) _____ together in elementary school.

6. By the end of the school semester, I (pass) _____ all of my exams.

7. She couldn't call her friend because she (lose) _____ his phone number.

8. She (just / reach) _____ home when it started to rain.

9. She (never / taste) _____ Japanese food before she went to Japan.

10. He (already / lose) _____ his glasses when he searched his backpack.

11. By the time the man left his house, the mall (already / close) _____.

12. As he walked in the door, I (just / finish) _____ reading my novel.

13. When I opened the refrigerator, I realized the milk (be) _____ there for a month.

14. I forgot to lock my house because I (leave) _____ quickly this morning.

15. The people who (arrive) _____ early left by 8:00 P.M.

Name _____ Date _____

EXERCISE 3 Fill in information about your own life and about people you know using the past perfect tense.

Example: I had *finished elementary school* _____ by 2000.

1. I had never _____ before high school.
2. By 2005, I had already _____.
3. Before last month I hadn't _____ because I was afraid.
4. My teacher had _____ before class ended.
5. By the time I finished my classwork, _____.

EXERCISE 4 Rewrite each sentence with the past perfect tense of the verb in parentheses.

Example: Ever since she was little, she (think) about being an accountant.
Ever since she was little, she *had thought about being an accountant*.

1. She (always / enjoy) math.

_____

2. She (always / want) to work in an office.

_____

3. She (decide) to enroll in an accounting course.

_____

4. She (forget) to register for the class.

_____

5. She (miss) the deadline for registration.

_____

6. She (see) the schedule for next term.

_____

7. She (not / see) any accounting course listed.

_____

8. She (ask) when the school would be offering another accounting course.

_____

9. Her guidance counselor (explain) to her that she would have to wait to register.

_____

10. She (wonder) if it would be too late to take the course next year.

_____

Name _____ Date _____

EXERCISE 5 Complete each sentence with the past perfect tense of the verb in parentheses.

Example: Shaine (leave) for school.
Shaine *had left* for school.

1. Shaine (walk) to school every day.

   _____

2. One morning, she (find) a key on the ground.

   _____

3. She (pick) it up.

   _____

4. Shaine (take) it to school with her.

   _____

5. She (think) about the key all day.

   _____

6. She (wonder) what the key was for.

   _____

7. She (see) her friend Leyla.

   _____

8. Leyla told Shaine that she (lose) the key to her locker.

   _____

9. Leyla explained that she (look) everywhere for it.

   _____

10. Shaine told Leyla that she (find) a key on her way to school.

    _____

11. Shaine (return) the key to Leyla.

    _____

EXERCISE 6 Write five sentences using the past perfect tense.

1. _____
2. _____
3. _____
4. _____
5. _____

Grammar Focus

Use with student text page 388.

Understand Modal Auxiliaries

LIST OF MODALS	FACTS ABOUT MODALS

can
 	
could
 	
should
 	
will
 	
would
 	
may
 	
might
 	
must
 	
(have to)
 	
(be able to)
	1. Modals are different from other verbs because they don't take an –*s*, –*ed*, or –*ing* ending:
	    He **can** drive. (not: He **cans** drive.)
	
	2. Modals are different from other verbs because we don't use an infinitive after a modal. We use the base form. Compare:
	    He wants **to leave.** He **must leave.**
	
	3. To form the negative, put *not* after the modal.
	    He **should not** drive.
	
	4. Some verbs are like modals in meaning: *have to, be able to:*
	    He **can** pay the rent = He **is able to** pay the rent.

WH–WORD	MODAL (+ *NOT*)	SUBJECT	MODAL (+ *NOT*)	MAIN VERB	COMPLEMENT	SHORT ANSWER
		Mario	**should**	study	English.	
		He	**shouldn't**	study	literature.	
	Should	he		study	grammar?	Yes, he **should.**
Why	**should**	he		study	grammar?	
Why	**shouldn't**	he		study	literature?	
		Who	**should**	study	literature?	

EXERCISE **1**   Underline the modals in each sentence below.

Example: You <u>must</u> be here by 9:00.

1. We shouldn't talk in class.

2. Do you have to play the music so loud?

3. I can write with my left hand.

4. I can understand French.

5. She might go tomorrow.

6. Why would we do this now?

7. There should be a sign somewhere.

8. We must turn left soon.

9. May we leave early today?
10. I should take an aspirin.

EXERCISE 2 Unscramble each group of words to write a statement.

Example: drive / she / can't _She can't drive._____

1. he / pen / can / use / a _____
2. she / eat / her / should / dinner _____
3. can't / they / swim _____
4. leave / Gloria / apartment / might / her _____
5. he / come / on Friday / may _____
6. do / it / you / could / in the morning _____
7. you / taking / will / be / notes _____
8. wouldn't / me / Alan / the secret / tell _____
9. my / may / mother / be / there _____
10. you / listen / me / to / must _____

EXERCISE 3 Unscramble each group of words to make a question.

Example: drive / she / can't _Can't she drive?_____

1. can / Spanish / you / speak _____
2. will / he / us / meet / there _____
3. should / I / buy / one _____
4. you / talk / must / so loudly _____
5. could / I / water / glass / of / have / a _____
6. pass / me / would / you / the / please / butter _____
7. sing / Marianne / can _____
8. the concert / with / couldn't / us / he / go / to _____
9. leave / a / shouldn't / we / tip _____
10. a store / won't / there / be / there _____

EXERCISE 4 Fill in each blank with *must* or *must not* to tell about laws in your city.

Example: You _____*must*_____ recycle your bottles and cans.

1. You _____ throw your garbage in the street.
2. You _____ pay your taxes.
3. You _____ buy a token to use the subway.
4. You _____ have a license to drive a car.
5. You _____ park in a no-parking zone.

EXERCISE 5 Fill in each blank with *have to* or *don't have to* to make true statements about your schedule. Remember that *don't have to* means *not necessary to*.

Example: I ____*have to*____ go to the post office today.

1. I _____ meet someone today.
2. I _____ make a call later.
3. I _____ wash the dishes now.
4. I _____ do laundry this week.
5. I _____ clean my room later.
6. I _____ write a composition.
7. I _____ take a test in this week.
8. I _____ go grocery shopping.
9. I _____ work today.
10. I _____ exercise today.

EXERCISE 6 Fill in each blank with a verb to tell what these people have to or don't have to do in these situations.

Example: My cat is hungry. I have to _____*feed*_____ it.

1. Martha's car is dirty. She has to _____ it.
2. Joseph is on vacation. He doesn't have to _____.
3. Alberto needs money. He must _____ a job.
4. Val and Henry are rich. They don't have to _____.
5. Sarah is a teacher. She must _____ homework to her students.
6. David is a student. He has to _____.
7. The party is casual. You don't have to _____.
8. I have a job interview tomorrow. I have to _____ a suit.
9. Katherine found someone's bag. She has to _____ it.
10. The teacher collected our compositions. He has to _____ them.
11. They are diabetic. They must not _____ sugar.
12. You drive a car. You must _____ an updated license.
13. He missed six classes already. He must not _____ another class.
14. The assignment was optional. You don't have to _____ it.
15. To prevent injury, all children must _____ seatbelts in a car.

EXERCISE 7 Write what you would say in each of the following situations in your class.

Examples: You want someone to spell a word for you.

Could you spell this, please?

You want to borrow some money.

May I borrow 5 dollars until tomorrow?

1. You want your teacher to repeat something.

_____

2. You want your teacher to speak more slowly.

_____

3. You want your teacher to speak louder.

_____

4. You want your teacher to explain something.

_____

5. You want to ask a question.

_____

6. You want to borrow some paper from a classmate.

_____

7. You want to use someone's dictionary.

_____

8. You want to borrow someone's eraser.

_____

9. You want a noisy classmate to be quiet.

_____

10. You want to join someone's group.

_____

Grammar Focus

Use with student text page 402.

Use Adverbs of Frequency

FREQUENCY WORD	FREQUENCY	EXAMPLE
always	100%	I **always** go running on Saturday morning.
usually	⇩	You **usually** join me at 8:00.
often	⇩	We were **often** tired after we ran.
sometimes	⇩	He **sometimes** had breakfast with friends.
rarely/seldom	⇩	She **rarely/seldom** runs in the winter.
never	0%	They **never** run in the snow.

LANGUAGE NOTES:
1. Frequency words come after the verb **be** but before other main verbs.
2. **Usually, often,** and **sometimes** can come at the beginning of a sentence.

EXERCISE 1 Choose the correct adverb. Fill in each bubble completely.

Example: I am never late to school. I am _____ on time.   ○ seldom ● always

1. I usually go to the library to study. I _____ study at home.   ○ often ○ rarely

2. Every Saturday and Sunday I sleep late. I _____ sleep late on weekends.   ○ never ○ always

3. Michel seldom gets enough time to study. He almost _____ needs more time.   ○ always ○ never

4. Luisa rarely organizes her work. She is _____ disorganized.   ○ seldom ○ usually

5. We always try to be quiet. We _____ disturb others.   ○ always ○ rarely

EXERCISE 2 Complete each sentence with the appropriate adverb.

Example: Marguerite _____ remembers Joe's birthday.   *always*

1. Marguerite is a thoughtful person. She _____ forgets anyone's birthday.   _____

2. She _____ sends her friends birthday cards.   _____

3. Her friends _____ forget hers either.   _____

4. They _____ send her cards, too.   _____

5. _____, they even buy each other small gifts.   _____

EXERCISE 3 Circle each adverb of frequency. Then rewrite each sentence using an adverb that is opposite in meaning.

Example: Sharon (seldom) finishes her homework.

Sharon *usually* finishes her homework. _____

1. Jasmine always reads.

   _____

2. Ryan never gets good grades.

   _____

3. Jasmine and Ryan seldom study together.

   _____

4. Sharon rarely does her homework.

   _____

5. Ryan is always late.

   _____

6. Jasmine is never early.

   _____

7. Sharon never raises her hand.

   _____

8. Ryan always hands in his homework.

   _____

9. Jasmine rarely speaks in class.

   _____

10. Sharon never helps other students in her class.

    _____

11. Ryan's responses are always correct.

    _____

12. Sharon seldom participates.

    _____

13. Jasmine never speaks to her friends.

    _____

14. Sharon rarely completes her assignments.

    _____

15. Ryan always passes his tests.

    _____

VISIONS Unit 6 • Chapter 4 It Could Still Be a Robot

EXERCISE 4 Use the adverb of frequency in each one of these sentences.

Example: The sun shines in the summer (usually)

The sun usually shines in the summer.

1. Flowers bloom in the spring. (always)

   _____

2. It rains in April. (often)

   _____

3. It is hot in February. (rarely)

   _____

4. It snows in August. (never)

   _____

5. It is windy in June. (seldom)

   _____

6. It is cold in November. (usually)

   _____

7. Trees bloom late. (sometimes)

   _____

EXERCISE 5 Unscramble each group of words to write a statement.

Example: often / Bailey / shopping / goes

Bailey often goes shopping.

1. clothes / usually / buys / Bailey

   _____

2. tries / on / first / always / them / she

   _____

3. coupons / she / sometimes / uses

   _____

4. seldom / buys / things / Bailey / on / sale

   _____

5. Bailey / shopping / often / with / goes / Tess

   _____

6. shopping / alone / goes / rarely / Tess

   _____

7. sometimes / Tess / CDs / buys

_____

8. pays / credit / card / Bailey / always / with / a

_____

9. cash / Tess / uses / seldom

_____

10. food / shopping / Bailey / never / and / Tess / go / together

_____

11. rarely / same / buy / things / Tess / Bailey / and / the

_____

EXERCISE 6 Write sentences about yourself using adverbs of frequency.

Example: (always) *I always get to school early.* _____

1. (always) _____
2. (often) _____
3. (sometimes) _____
4. (rarely) _____
5. (never) _____

EXERCISE 7 Write sentences about a friend using adverbs of frequency.

Example: (usually) *Daniel is usually reliable.* _____

1. (always) _____
2. (usually) _____
3. (sometimes) _____
4. (seldom) _____
5. (never) _____

VISIONS **Unit 6 • Chapter 4** It Could Still Be a Robot

VISIONS A Grammar Practice • Copyright © Thomson Heinle